Hummingbirds and Kaleidoscopes

Copyright © Lucy Picksley 2024

All rights reserved.

No part of this book may be reproduced, distributed, stored in a retrieval system, or transmitted in any form or by any means, electronic, mechanical, photocopying, recording, or otherwise, without express written permission of the publisher.

ISBN: 9798324446369

Written by: Kathryn Hall—www.cjhall.co.uk
Cover art: Louise Wilson—www.thirteenoclock.co
Formatting: Catherine Arthur—www.catherinearthur.com

For Haydn, for his endless faith.
Brady, for his unbelievable bravery.
For Mark, because the wait was worthwhile.
I love you all.

Foreword

by Sarah Maskell MBE FCIPD CCMI RAF

Without a hesitation, being asked to write a foreword for this incredible book is in the top few of my proudest moments. From watching Lucy blossom in these last few years, and having had the privilege of sharing some of her knowledge first hand, I feel a connection to the rollercoaster of emotions that have been invested into every word, story and memory. I truly hope that you have prepared yourself for the waves of warmth, mindfulness and reflection that will emerge from the following pages and chapters.

Looking beyond the words in this book to the glorious patterns and fabrics that Lucy has designed and developed, I know that the ideas and drawings, turning into calculations and measurements, have created a huge mosaic of special memories. As a mother myself I also know that as Lucy shares how her life has been shaped and her children have grown, her legacy will keep growing as more lovely sewists get involved, more items are sewn and adored, and new followers join and add to the family.

It seems so long ago but I first met Lucy when I asked a neighbour if she knew anyone who would be a knowledgeable sewing teacher, as I wanted to move beyond curtain hems. What I didn't know was the impact that this wonderful woman would have on my ability to seek enjoyment and not just refuge in my sewing. When I went along for my first class I had recently retired from the military, moved home and was grappling with the realities of change. From the very first moment I saw the huge smile and heard the welcoming words of Lucy, I felt safe in the space to learn. Lucy really did show me that 'sewing gives you hope'.

From hand stitches and threading a machine through the complexities of button holes and French seams, it was like Lucy could understand that I needed time for my brain to seek solitude and rest while my hands were busy making something. I embarked on a few pieces and with the support of Lucy I tried new ideas, new designers, and new fabrics. It is such a proud moment to put the TV on and see Lucy sharing a new design, or follow her on her socials knowing that without hesitation I could drop her a message and her calming presence would be right by my side.

I am humbled to have gained a friend, and a teacher, for sewing and for life.

Enjoy the book (you may need a supply of tea and tissues).

Chapter One

I used to have a fabric dolly. She was a battered old thing but I adored her. She had a long string that allowed me to hang her from my dressing gown hanger on the back of my bedroom door. My room was tiny and I had a white and grey cabin bed to give me extra space for my things. But dolly always stayed right there, where I could keep an eye on her when I was in bed, because she held the key to my fortunes ...
"Redcar Wallet"

One of my favourite pastimes as a young girl was to climb to the top of Newbold Comyn, lie on my side with my arms folded securely across my chest, and let the adrenaline take over as my twin brothers would nudge me over, pushing me down the hill whilst I screamed in delight. I would roll over and over, waiting to land at the bottom with an almighty giggle and a determination to climb back to the top. I was a child with nothing to worry about and so much to look forward to. It was a carefree adventure, escapism that would stay with me into adulthood, an overwhelming feeling of being young and free and only having one thing to think about right at that very moment as the world would spin around me. 'Me next,' one of my brothers would shout as I'd reach the top again before watching the world spin around him instead.

Lucy Picksley

I grew up in Warwick with my parents and my older twin brothers, in what I will always treasure as our family home. There was a pond in our front garden that would enchant me as a magnificent cherry blossom tree would hang over it, almost touching the water and leaving petals floating on the surface when spring arrived, bringing new life to our ever-changing sanctuary. In the back garden was a pear tree that produced the most delicious fruit for us to pick, and my dad would lift us up to take one from the branch which he would then cut into and offer a slice to each of us. I can still taste those pears today, and I remember his face when handing us a slice so we could savour its sweetness and give our approval of family moments together.

The gate in the back garden led onto the playground at the back of our school and my brothers and I would use it as a shortcut. Rose bushes grew in many of the front gardens on our street and my friend Roxy and I would pick them and put them in jars that our mums had saved, then fill the jars with water and make our own rose perfume. Even in those days of my childhood, I was only happy if I was doing something creative, making something from scratch, and hoping that one day I would take my creativity to a whole new level. I suppose, as a child, I hoped our old washed out jam jars of rose petal perfume would one day be manufactured and sold in High Street stores. Everything feels so achievable when you're a child, the world at your fingertips, hopes and dreams just around the corner. And then age catches up with us as we sit exams and go to college, find a job and perhaps achieve so much more than being enchanted by blossom trees and roses trapped in a jar. Roxy and I would wait patiently before eventually removing the lids and inhaling the earthy scent of our homemade creation. It was the excitement of what we might breathe in that was the best part, for the actual experience once the jar gaped open to reveal petals still floating in water wasn't quite as enthralling as we'd hoped.

In 1986, we moved to Lillington and lived in a lovely semi-detached house on a road that led to my primary school. My brothers got the largest room and I took the box room, which I didn't mind, of course, and when my younger brother Toke came along, I guess I was extremely lucky to have kept that space to myself. It was a surprise for Mum and Dad, but a welcome addition to our family, now of six.

I had a best friend when I lived there called Kath and we'd walk to school together, though most mornings she was late leaving her house because her mum insisted on putting her hair into pigtails, and the fact it was always so knotted up meant a simple task turned into a drama that warranted us having to rush to get to school before the bell sounded. Another friend, Suzie, who lived next door to me, would join us occasionally too, and we'd spend many happy hours playing French skipping where we'd tie a length of elastic around chair legs so we could play doubles. Perhaps one of the most poignant memories I have of those childhood days is of my mum, me and Suzie, sat in a row on our green sofa, whilst Mum taught us how to knit. Little did I know back then that in my future I would be an expert knitter, making my own clothes and using my creative skills to earn a living. I have so much to be thankful for, not least my mum's patience every time I dropped a stitch!

It was several years later, in 2003, after life had given me a few lemons and I decided to make lemonade that I met my soulmate and future husband, Mark. People ask, including me once upon a time, whether we believe in love at first sight. I can honestly say, with hand on heart, that yes, *I do*. And I went on to say those two little words the following year when Mark and I made our vows and pledged to spend the rest of our lives together, come what may. I fell deeply in love with him from the moment I met him. I knew we would always be together, propping each other up should any storms threaten our blue sky, and I remember feeling in the first six months of our relationship how incredibly lucky I was to have found my wonderful life partner.

We did everything together, visited different places, stayed in cheap B&Bs just so we could snatch as much time alone as possible without anyone needing our attention from elsewhere. We talked about everything and anything, shared our dreams and explored each other's worlds to the point where we knew one hundred per cent that those two worlds had now been undoubtedly fused together. I'd had a rough few years previous to meeting Mark and had chosen never to discuss it with anyone, but he brought my fears into the open and made me realise that I could tell him anything and share all the bad points just as much as I could share the good ones. Our love knew no bounds, and still doesn't, after twenty years of marriage.

It wasn't all plain sailing and a bed of roses in those early years of marriage, however, as Mark and I experienced much heartache when I discovered I'd had a miscarriage. I was twenty-five and even though I hadn't realised I was pregnant when it happened, it was a tremendous loss knowing I could have been nurturing a baby that just wasn't meant to be. We were incredibly happy and the love we had for each other was enough to help us come to terms with the upset. People assume you'll get over it and go on to conceive again, and I was thrilled, if not apprehensive, when that did finally happen. But when I lost that baby too, it made me realise those carefree days of making rose petal perfume and taking a shortcut over the school playground were well and truly behind me. I had to face these fears now, be a grown-up and ask myself why this had happened a second time. It goes without saying it was a very difficult time for both Mark and I, and several months later I went to Spain for a week with my parents to try and get away from the morbidity of real life and worrying about my future dreams of hopefully becoming a mother.

On one of the days we were in Spain, we travelled high up into the mountains to the top of Mount Roel where we visited the stunning 18th Century monastery of the Virgen del Saliente. Its ancient stone façade with traditional Spanish turrets seemed to take me away to another world where only tranquillity and divinity resided; where I was once more in my land of escapism, inhaling the rose petals and the fresh air that surrounded me. I closed my eyes and stood still for a while, thinking about how my life had taken such a drastic turn in just a matter of months; remembering how happy I was on my honeymoon in the beautiful town of Tsilivi on the Greek Island of Zakynthos. Such bittersweet memories were filling my mind as I tried desperately to clear the devastation of loss. But those feelings suddenly became overtaken by thoughts of Mark, my soulmate and my beloved husband, at home on his own, living through the same nightmare I'd been living through. I knew there and then that I had to leave, go back to my best friend and continue our lifelong dreams together. I'd never needed anyone more in my life than I needed him at that moment, and the day we were due to fly back to England couldn't come quick enough.

Mount Roel changed me that day and reminded me that life would always go on, no matter what happened to us. I would face my fears and move forward to begin again, reconnect with my inner-self and allow my hopes and dreams to resurface. Perhaps the mountain was speaking to me in many ways, telling me things were going to change from now on and that I needed to try as much as I could to put the heartache behind me for the sake of my family. For, little did I know, I was pregnant again, and this time I would go full-term and give birth to our first son, Brady, whom I brought into the world in 2006.

I still think about rolling down Newbold Comyn with my older brothers and feeling that euphoria I felt back then as a child, the carefree adventures and the never-ending journeys into a fairy-tale world of dreams and ambitions and wanting nothing more than to climb back to the top and start the journey down all over again. One day, I will take my husband to the top of that hill and we will roll down together, embraced in each other's arms, just the two of us in our own little escapism as the world spins around us and encourages us to once more climb back to the top.

Chapter Two

A stunning kaleidoscope turned and polished from the most beautiful of woods. How could I not love and cherish it? To my eye I would place it as I looked through the small viewfinder, inside an abundance of bright colours that danced and moved with each motion of my hands. Mirrors encouraging the duplication of images, colours reverberating and escalating as they bounce off each other. The kaleidoscope, bringing me images of a child's face that is mesmerised by beauty in such simplicity ...
"Kaleidoscope"

My cats are very dear to me and my old faithful feline called Moon, hardly ever left my side when I was carrying Brady. It was as though she felt a need to protect my unborn baby and perhaps a need to protect me, too. Being pregnant wasn't the best experience I've ever had, probably because of the constant anxiety after having two miscarriages. I was always exhausted and ill with cold symptoms, and naturally became run down. Then, in the early hours of 16th February 2006, I started to feel the first contractions and assuming I most likely had plenty of time to go before this new baby would make an appearance, I got up and had a bath. Things calmed down for a while and after a second bath, Mark and I agreed it was time to head to Lincoln County Hospital Maternity Unit and get checked in.

I was examined and things were definitely moving along, but being in a room on the maternity ward was making me feel more anxious and so I made a rash suggestion to Mark that we go to the local Tesco superstore and have a walk around — my thoughts being that if nothing else, it would help speed up the imminent birth. Mark parked up and we walked slowly into the store, me waddling along and my ever-faithful husband supporting me up. The first aisle just in the main entrance contained crates of peppers; red, green, orange and yellow, and it took all my strength to get past them. The contractions were getting stronger and as I leaned against those crates for what seemed like the hundredth time, Mark put his foot down and insisted we go back to the hospital. Looking back in hindsight, it wasn't the best suggestion I'd ever made to go wandering around a supermarket when I was so close to giving birth!

We got back to the maternity unit where I was examined again and had endless cups of tea brought to me, none of which I drank, something which Mark still talks and laughs about today. It was 4.57pm when my first born made his appearance, and I'd gone through the whole process without having any pain relief whatsoever. I felt like a warrior as I cradled my beautiful boy in my arms, wrapped in a pale blue hospital blanket, and felt like I was drowning in love. Mark rang our parents and gave them the good news, only telling them that the "baby" had been born, and when they all arrived at the hospital, still unaware of our baby's gender, I remember announcing to our parents as they all stood together that the name we had chosen was Brady. 'That's lovely,' my mum said. 'But is it a boy or a girl?' It made me laugh when she asked that; obviously we'd chosen a name for either gender. Had he been a girl, "she" would have been named Katy Elizabeth.

He was a model baby and hit all the usual milestones at the right time. His only health issue back then was an intolerance to baby formula, but that was soon rectified by a switch to soya milk. He loved bath time, splashing his little hands in the water, playing with toys and then having soothing cuddles whilst wrapped in his baby towel. Once we started him on solid food, it became evident that his favourite meal was fish pie. As I imagined, he really took to our pets—two cats and a rabbit—and Moon was particularly good with him. He adored her, though that wasn't difficult to do. He was sitting up by the age of six months and though we wondered how long it would be until he started crawling, by the time he was eleven months old, he stood up and just started to walk. The time had come to move ornaments and rearrange the furniture somewhat to prevent accidents, but away he went, making us wonder why we'd ever worried about the lack of crawling in the first place.

He was six months old when I returned to work and we arranged a mixture of childcare. Our parents helped out and he went to a nursery nearby also, but even at such a young age, it seemed it was difficult for him to settle and so we moved him to a different nursery after a short while. By the time Brady started primary school, he'd been to various nurseries, none of which had really helped. He never seemed to fit in to any of them, his needs appearing more demanding than perhaps the average baby or toddler. We saw he'd become agitated and upset, the staff would report to us that his behaviour needed checking, and obviously this gave us cause for concern. One nursery he went to was an establishment attached to a private school. Their ethos was more of a traditional learning method, and we did notice a difference in him for a while, as though things were starting to settle down and perhaps it was what he'd needed all along. But unfortunately, it became apparent that he just wasn't connecting or bonding with the staff, and we reluctantly came to the realisation that although the nursery's routine and structure was what Brady needed, it wasn't the right place for him to learn in these early years of his life. We were, as you can imagine, frustrated by the whole thing and we just had to hope that when he finally started primary school, things would take a turn for the better, that he would settle down, and we could stop worrying. The guilt I felt during those years was phenomenal. Moving him to different nurseries and expecting him to make new friends, connect with the assistants whilst Mark and I worked to give our little family a good life, not to mention giving Brady a good start, really was taking its toll. But the day finally came when I dropped him off on his first day at school and allowed myself a sigh of relief with the desperate hope that this would be the making of him.

Brady was, and still is, a very bright boy. He did well at school and we felt happy that he was learning and coming home with new reading books and reports saying he'd done well in the classroom. For a child of five, it's a long day, and naturally he would be exhausted and ready for something to eat when he got in, all very normal behaviour for our son. But within a few short months, I was called into school and told he was displaying behaviour that wasn't in-keeping for a neuro-typical child, and it was then that we were first introduced to the term "Special Educational Needs", or "SEN" for short. His needs were to be monitored more closely as staff would watch out for any further signs that would indicate there could be something more going on than just a young child being unable to settle. It was during his third year of primary education, that we once more had the task of finding a new establishment for him to attend as he'd become visibly unhappy and again portrayed an indication that he wasn't fitting in.

We found a place for him in a little village school where the maximum class size was fifteen. There, he would get more one-to-one attention and hopefully be able to make a friend or two. It was noticed, much to our relief, that he began to excel, and his academic skills were being recognised. All good, until I was called into the school and told to sit down.

'It's not what he says,' the teacher told me, 'but the way he says it.' As his parents, we knew what she meant, and even now, at the age of eighteen, we still pull him up on it occasionally, though as an adult, of course, rather than a young boy.

When Brady was five, and going through the first throes of his education where his special needs were becoming apparent, I gave birth to our second son, Haydn George. I'd had another miscarriage before falling pregnant with Haydn, so to have another baby, and a healthy one at that, felt like a miracle. Things were somewhat different with Haydn during the birth, as I went through it alone. I was admitted to hospital for an induction as my placenta was failing, something that would obviously have been extremely dangerous to both of us. They went ahead with the induction and within hours I started to feel contractions. The nurse on the ward told me I wouldn't be experiencing contractions for another few days, and didn't seem particularly worried about me. I had to stay in hospital, of course, though on a general ward rather than the maternity unit, and tried hard to lie down and get myself settled on the bed. But another hour or two later I was again pressing the emergency button and trying to make them believe that I was indeed having contractions. I needed to use the bathroom and was helped by a nurse. It wasn't ideal because it was evening and Mark wasn't allowed to visit at that time. They'd sent him home earlier, adamant that no baby would appear for a while yet.

But I knew differently; I'd already had a baby and knew the signs of how contractions felt. I knew my own body, yet I felt no one was listening. Having got relief from two baths when I was in labour with Brady, I decided to go back to the bathroom, which seemed like a mile-walk down the corridor but was probably, in reality, about fifteen metres away. There, I put the plug in the bath and turned on the taps. The relief I felt when I immersed myself into the water was palpable; it was exactly the right thing for me to have done at that time. I lay in that bath for about two hours until, eventually, I knew things were getting more severe at the business end and it was paramount that someone helped me out and started taking me seriously. I pulled the emergency cord and very soon a nurse burst into the bathroom.

'This baby is coming!' I said, determined that she wouldn't just brush it off again. Her reply was to tell me to get out of the bath and she'd examine me. It was something, I suppose, and as she left the room, I slowly hauled myself up and somehow managed to climb out of the bath, clutching my over-inflated stomach and landing on the tiled floor on top of a bath mat. The moment both my feet touched the floor, Haydn made his debut into the world, sliding out and leaving me in a crouched position. It was a strange and potentially frightening way to be first introduced to my second born, but it was a wonderful moment all the same, and I think that because I was completely alone when I gave birth to him, it made our bond extra special.

The nurses, of course, were somewhat in shock at what had happened, and perhaps realised then that they should have listened to me. But all I was bothered about was the fact Mark hadn't witnessed his son being brought into the world and it left me upset for him. It was when the nurse had left the bathroom after telling me to get out of the bath that she rang him to say nothing was happening but that she did feel I needed him with me. Being of the understanding that I was perfectly okay and could have been laid up on that ward for days before being taken to the delivery suite in the maternity unit, Mark nonchalantly made his way to the hospital, calling for fuel on the way, not at all worried about me as he'd been assured his wife was absolutely fine. He eventually arrived on the ward and because it was out of visiting hours, he told a passing nurse who he was and that he'd been asked to come in to keep me company for a while.

'Oh, congratulations on the birth of your son, Mr Picksley,' the nurse said. Suffice to say, Mark was particularly disappointed to find out that I'd already given birth and he hadn't been there for me. That really upset him, perhaps more than it did me, and I don't think either of us can ever forgive the staff on that ward for not listening to me when I told them I was very close to having my baby.

My blue-eyed boy, Haydn, and I, still have the special bond we had in those first few minutes of his life. He's a teenager now and full of hormones and cheek. But he's also an angel and makes us laugh all the time, and I love that about him so very much. He's been through a lot in his short life with his older brother, watching him have meltdowns and often being at the wrong end of them. But he adores Brady; the love he has for him is fierce and he never complains or fights back when Brady has one of his bad days. He holds me when I'm feeling vulnerable and shows a steadfast strength of character whenever I get to the point where I show weakness. He reassures me that everything will be okay and I always believe him, because I know he will always be there for all of us, whatever happens. He sometimes reminds me that when things are tough for his older brother, it isn't Brady so much as the autism making him that way, and that's incredibly comforting to hear those words coming from the mouth of a boy who sounds so much like a grown-up.

Haydn was very different as a young child and his early-years care once I went back to work was completely the opposite to what we experienced with Brady. Haydn threw himself into his nursery days and made friends quickly. His imagination impressed everyone around him and he was always so keen to talk to people, not just other children, but staff, too. He talked a lot and had a great fascination with trains, and he developed a very close friendship with my friend's son, Hudson, who he's still friends with today. My two children from the same parents, yet so different in many ways.

Brady became more challenging as he got older, and his years in primary school weren't easy for any of us. We were called into school often to discuss his behaviour and even though his teachers knew something was wrong, they refused to refer our boy for a SEN assessment. His issues were obvious for anyone to see and we just needed help to get us along what was now turning into an extremely tough road ahead.

Eventually, at the age of eleven, he moved up to secondary school and we wondered if things would improve there, if perhaps there would be a better system, one which would offer the help he so desperately needed. But by his second week of being at that school, I answered a phone call from the headmistress, Miss Brace, who voiced her concerns about my eldest son, needing to discuss these as a matter of urgency. I knew, when I hung up the phone that day, that she knew what was going on with Brady. She would have seen many children with special needs throughout her career, and from the tone in her voice I was quite sure she knew what we had been, and still were, going through. That phone call led to the most important meeting of our lives when Miss Brace called a gathering with local authority workers and the school's special educational needs coordinator, also known as SENCO. At that time,

Brady had been living between our house and my mum's, sometimes to give us all some space as a family, and other times because we just weren't getting on, and that, as his parents, we just felt like we were failing him. Staying at my mum's helped him a little in so far as a change of scenery was necessary, and of course it helped Mark and I, not to mention Haydn, to heave a sigh of relief and have a little respite.

At long last, a plan was put in place and things started to move in the right direction that would help Brady, mainly in an educational setting. He was assigned an Early Help worker called Leanne, who worked with him on his emotional welfare needs thus trying to make him understand what was happening to him. A Statement of Special Educational Needs was drawn up and the school was allocated a small increase in their special needs budget for some one-to-one tuition. At that age, it's difficult for any child to understand the world around them, accept the natural changes that will occur as they enter puberty and start to grow. In many ways, Brady needed to engage with himself, learn about his inner-child and realise that the behaviour he exhibited wasn't always acceptable or "normal", for want of a better word, to that of his peers. The positive aspect in all this was that the school and local authority were actually doing something to help him and we could hope better things were on the horizon for our eldest son.

Brady was later diagnosed as being on the threshold for Autism Spectrum Disorder. This diagnosis included various conditions: Kanner Syndrome, Asperger Syndrome, Pathological Demand Avoidance, and Attention Deficit Hyperactivity Disorder, also known as ADHD. These conditions are real and the diagnosis was only the beginning of Brady's story. He wasn't a "naughty" boy or a "disruptive" one; he had an alternative character that warranted extra-curricular activities, help, understanding, and a lot of patience. We felt we were finally getting somewhere. But the help he needed still wasn't forthcoming and was proving almost impossible for us to secure. He went through what we classed as a "state of crisis" and yet CAMHS (Child and Adolescent Mental Health Services) still refused our applications to have him referred.

Our family has been the main source of help that Brady has received; me, Mark, our parents, and of course, Haydn. We've helped him grow and watched him have meltdowns that have scared us all, not just on Brady's behalf, but ours, too. We've had to accept over the years that our beautiful boy, now a young man, will never be like his neuro-typical peers, or indeed his younger brother, and while that's affected us deeply in so many ways, we love him unconditionally and have come to terms with the fact our lives will go on, perhaps somewhat differently to others', but we will always have each other.

The first ten years of my marriage to Mark was nothing short of a challenge. But we knew we could get through it because we were together, learning as we went along. Bringing our boys up has given us both the strength to get through anything as we hold each other's hand and tread this path that has become our own journey into what could perhaps be classed as the unknown. We nurtured our sons when they were babies and gave them the space they needed when they started to grow. And despite Brady's complexities and Haydn's reassurance, we know that our path will continue to have its twists and turns and will probably one day bring us something else to test our family unit.

Chapter Three

I left home at the age of sweet sixteen to live with my gran in the south of England and there I studied art. It was then that I started to form my own identity; wearing the clothing I wanted to wear and cutting and colouring my hair without the worry of fitting in. With that sense of freedom and letting go of conformity, my inner spirit materialised and I knew it had always been there within me ... "Maiden"

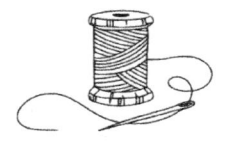

In 2012, when Haydn was just a year old and Brady was in primary school, I knew it was important amidst everything going on that I needed to find some escapism somewhere and occasionally just wander off into my own world where everything was *normal*. My love of sewing from a young age had never left me and as I hadn't sewn anything for many years, it suddenly became important to pick up a needle and thread again and create something. I thought about what that could be and decided, after much deliberation, it would be a dress. It felt as though it was something I needed to do; start sewing a garment that would give me something else to think about apart from my two sons' constant needs. I had no idea at that time how important making a dress would be to my future, but I set about, making notes and lists and searching for the perfect fabric. I chose Kaffe Fassett fabric and gave the design invisible zips with darts front and back. It was princess seamed and quite beautiful. I spent many evenings sitting at the dining table, studying the pattern and all the technicalities involved, trying to make sense of the terms and odd-looking symbols, many that I had to research to understand what they meant. There were instructions on how to make a dart on the pattern, but back then I didn't even know what a dart was, never mind how to make one. I was lucky that a good friend helped me learn and I was eventually able to complete my first project before moving on to the next one.

The start of my sewing journey, albeit as a hobby, had begun, and when I hung the dress up on a coat hanger and took a few steps back from it, I looked on in admiration at what I had produced, not just at the garment itself, but at the fact I had achieved something that meant so much to me apart from being a mother to my two boys. Mark was hugely impressed and as I stood in front of him and gave him a twirl, I'm sure the pride in his expression matched that in mine.

Buying different patterns became a really exciting prospect in those days as I started to learn and make sense of not only my new hobby of sewing, but also this new me; someone who wasn't spending every waking moment worrying about special educational needs and baby formula, and instead was enjoying doing something creative that left me feeling like my days had been filled in so many delightful ways. I'd often buy the wrong types of fabric in those early days and end up mismatching patterns to the material, which would be extremely frustrating. But it only added to the challenge I'd set myself, and even though some of the garments I went on to make didn't fit perfectly when I first started out, I didn't care. My ambition to make clothes far outweighed the exasperation of thinking I'd finished yet another garment only to realise I'd bought the wrong buttons or hadn't lined up the stitching properly. I just wanted to make things, and it was particularly important to me to learn the technical elements of my craft.

It got to the point where I felt I didn't need to think about seeking a little escapism anymore, because sewing became the therapy that I had subconsciously craved perhaps longer than I dared to admit. It was my new-found hobby, and I couldn't get enough of it. I'd often get up early on a Sunday morning, before the boys or Mark were awake, and watch Create and Craft TV channel, a television show not dissimilar to Sewing Street. Rather than buy their patterns, I'd make endless notes in a notebook, writing down their tips and advice and listening to what they, as experts, were recommending. I was able to learn such a lot from them back then, drowning myself in knowledge that I would go on to use when it came to creating my own designs. The presenters on that show inspired me and gave me the much-needed guidance that I sought as a hobby sewist, perhaps a part of me knowing back then that one day I could be taking this a lot more seriously. Before long, I made a pinafore dress for my friend's little girl, a gorgeous item made from a mixture of Jemima Puddleduck and a Rose and Hubble ditsy print design, and I added an adorable heart-shaped pocket in the front that she used to keep her tiny treasures in. I was so proud to see little Frankie modelling that dress for me, more inspiration that encouraged me to carry on.

The family came first, of course, Mark, Brady and Haydn, and the issues were still ongoing with Brady as meetings were held at school to discuss his extra needs. But even though it was hard trying to get through each day knowing how much we had to deal with, sewing helped me cope better and took my thoughts to a new place where I could put things in order and remove some of the chaos that was permanently clogging up our everyday lives.

The sewing became so important to me that after a while I decided to go one step further and create my own wardrobe—make all my own clothes by buying fabrics and the materials and working from my own designs. Rather than buying ready-made clothes from a shop, I'd visit fabric stores and get to work, making items that would be a perfect fit instead of being a bit too big in one area and a bit too tight in another. It's difficult to find the perfect garment in a shop unless you aren't bothered about a budget, but this meant I could have a wardrobe filled with my favourite fabrics and designs and clothes that would look like they'd been made especially for me. Which, of course, they had; by my own fair hands.

I loved it whenever someone asked where I'd bought my dress, or want to know where I'd got that blouse from, as my answer was a very proud, 'I made it myself.' People became interested in "how" I made my clothes, where I bought the materials from, how long it took, was it easy, difficult, fiddly or frustrating. But to me, it wasn't any of those things. It was something I didn't just *want* to do but became an area of my life that I *needed* to do, and that gave me so much encouragement to keep going.

Hummingbirds and Kaleidoscopes

It was four years later, in 2016, when I was encouraged to undertake a qualification known as PTLLS — Preparing to Teach in the Lifelong Learning Sector — and then I accepted a freelance position with CLIP, Community Learning in Partnership. I'd been working with the organisation since 2010 in a programme aimed at tackling youth unemployment, but as things were beginning to wrap up and my role was inevitably going to become obsolete, I moved into the position of Resident Involvement Officer at a social housing organisation. There, I was later given a promotion to Community Engagement Co-ordinator where my duties involved helping people enhance their skills and improve their general outlook. This was something I really became committed to. My appetite to get out there and do the job to the best of my ability was overwhelming, and I couldn't wait to start.

I was given a budget to purchase materials to use for my pupils and I set about trawling shops and craft centres where I would marvel at the vast array of items on display; fabrics, ribbons, pompom trims and buttons. It was up to me what I chose and I always went for material that I knew would stand out and make people want to feel encouraged and eager to learn. My classes were run on a Saturday morning and even though I had to fill in mountains of paperwork, that sometimes felt somewhat ridiculous when all I wanted to do was teach eager students how to sew, I got on with the tasks in hand and made my job fun.

For four hours each week I helped people set up their machines and taught them the basics; the whys and wherefores of how to start. We'd lay fabrics together on a bench, cutting, snipping, turning and pressing, creating flags on a string, and one I remember vividly had the word "Dom" sewn across it, short for Dominic, which a lady hung over her son's bed. Another lady brought a range of *Doctor Who* fabric in and I helped her piece it all together to make a "Whovian-themed" bunting on a string for her daughter to fix to her bedroom wall. To see people's faces light up when creations had been completed was massively rewarding. I'd helped them fulfil something they'd probably wanted to do for years, yet needed guidance and some tutoring to put their ambitions to fruition.

The following year, my sewing and my role as a teacher were going well, but things at home were reaching breaking point and no matter how much I tried to escape from the everyday routine of being a parent to two boys and a wife to Mark, I knew that deep down the cracks were starting to appear within me. I was shuffling too much in my mind, always on the go, wanting to fix everything and take care of everyone, frustrated when I'd get a glimpse of realisation that sometimes, however much I persevered, I was just banging my head against a brick wall. I started writing a diary, another outlet that could maybe offer me therapy and a different way of looking at things. I'd open my wardrobe and look at the vast array of clothes I'd made, running my hand over each garment and remembering how I'd stitched and threaded and measured and smiled when they'd hung before me in all their glory. But they became just clothes, hanging before me as my enthusiasm began to wane.

In 2018, now two years after starting my work with CLIP, I ran a four-week workshop where my students had to make a patchwork cushion with applique lettering at the top that either read "LOVE" or "HOME". I had to follow a Scheme of Works, an official document which outlined the objectives of what my students needed to achieve by the time they had finished the course. It was hard work, albeit enjoyable to see people's faces light up as they began to learn, and as the courses I taught were cheap, it made it easier for anyone interested in learning to attend as they didn't have to fork out expensive fees. For people on certain benefits, the course was free. It had a varied range of attendees, some who knew nothing at all about sewing but were just interested to learn, and others who were determined to make something creative. Friendships were made and I saw how much pleasure some of the students were getting while mixing with others, perhaps having a few hours' escapism from an otherwise busy life of bringing up a family or working too hard throughout the week.

Having to manage a wide range of skills, and in some cases no skills, was incredibly difficult. Those who were absolute beginners tended to take most of my time, needing more help than those who were more familiar with a needle and thread. For me, I just wanted to help them all and make sure each and every person on my courses went away with a satisfied smile and feeling fulfilled. Their achievements were also mine, because I was very aware that without my help they might not have had the opportunity to learn this skill.

When I was visited by an OFSTED inspector one day, that was probably the start of the rise in my anxiety. I'd already been observed by an inspector in my first year with CLIP, so I should have known how things would go, what I'd be expected to do and say. But this particular time, Miss Ofsted arrived at my workshop and hovered in the background whilst I welcomed the students into the classroom and preached about the usual jargon of health and safety, before going through the itinerary and the objectives of what that session would entail. I was nervous, of course, and tried not to keep glancing at Miss Ofsted to gauge her reactions. We switched the sewing machines on and laid out fabrics and patterns and other materials that would be used, and just as we were going to start, one of the students, a lady who was a complete beginner, arrived late carrying a huge box containing a brand new sewing machine. She hadn't even opened the box, thinking it would be best to bring it to the workshop and have me show her from scratch how to use it. I couldn't believe it; this was a really important session for me to make a great impression and now I was expected to teach the one student who, incidentally, had been the one who often demanded the bulk of my time. Why now? I couldn't help thinking!

But the lady was eager to learn and I was eager to teach, and so between us, we set her new machine up and I somehow got her started on stitching a few pieces of fabric together. That session was one of the hardest for me because not only was I desperately trying to make Miss Ofsted see how capable I was, I also had to run from student to student, helping, teaching, and advising, while at the same time spending as much time as possible with Miss New Sewing Machine! I got through it, as did she and the rest of the class, and I was thrilled to get a glowing report at the end of the session saying I'd done incredibly well with no recommendations for me to make improvements. There was, however, a suggestion that the organisation considered how mixed the skill levels were in the class as I'm sure Miss Ofsted had seen how difficult it was for just one tutor to teach all these people of different capabilities, not to mention the lady with the new machine. It was an advisory to make sure there was adequate support in future that would assist a large class of varying skills.

But after that session, it made me realise that I didn't want to continue in this role. I was being dictated to by people who didn't really know much about the varying skillset and the challenges that posed. I was also spending an inordinate amount of time on paperwork, which I always felt was unnecessary when all people wanted to do was learn a craft. I wanted to help these people and I took great pleasure in doing that, but the system and its red tape and bureaucracy was eating into my time far too much. Having to go through the health and safety rules every week, and instructions on what to do in the event of a fire alarm was something else that was taking up too much time, valuable time that my students just wanted to spend learning how to sew. And then, of course, there were the inspections that made me feel intimidated somewhat, as though I was being tested when I knew in my heart that the job I did was of a high standard. My students always seemed happy when they left the class, and I always made sure that if they had any questions they should ask them and not feel obliged to just leave once we'd wrapped up and turned the machines off.

I knew at that point that I wanted to go solo. I needed to offer workshops for people that only I would be in charge of, sessions that were solely organised by me. And that led me to my next challenge of how I would make that dream come true.

Chapter Four

To be like Alice is what I set out to achieve. Though from my early years and into my twenties, I was quiet, cautious, and feeling pretty unsure about what I wanted from life. Later, I went down a rabbit hole to search out my identity, feeling brave and bold with a renewed sense of purpose, and even though being quiet is still a part of who I am, being unafraid and able to stand up for my beliefs no longer hinders my inner-child ...
"Alice"

In the early days, when my sewing journey began after making my beautiful Kaffe Fassett dress, I realised that it didn't just need to be garments I'd create, but items for the home, too. I wasn't too bothered back then about the actual item I made but more about the actual craft, the skill, and the creation of each design. I made small objects such as tool caddies, patchwork blankets, and notebook covers, and in 2013, I produced an odd-shaped cushion that was supposed to look like an owl. I have to admit it was the dodgiest-looking owl I'd ever seen, but I didn't care; I knew I had a lot to learn where choosing the right fabric was concerned, not to mention putting the design together. My enthusiasm was probably exhausting for poor Mark as even though I would never neglect my duties as a mum or indeed his wife, I couldn't get enough of this amazing new hobby I'd become so engrossed in.

But Mark being Mark, could see how determined I was to make a real go of this sewing lark and he found me an old desk with three drawers each side for me to use. It was just for me, and I loved it. He painted it for me in chalk paints of French grey and lavender and I trawled the internet to find drawer handles that would be totally in-keeping with my *Alice in Wonderland* obsession. Each handle had an image on it of the characters from the story, and it all made me feel like Alice herself; curious and desperate to know what happens next. Perhaps if I were to meet my own Mad Hatter and white rabbit, I would ponder on whether to give up and walk away because the project I'd been working on hadn't been what I'd envisaged—a little like the odd-shaped owl cushion. Or maybe I'd take a deep breath, put the dodgy designs behind me, and move on to bigger and better things. Of course, I've known the answer to that all along. Throwing the towel in never has been in my nature, and I know for definite it never will be.

Mark and I carried the desk upstairs to our bedroom and positioned it next to the window where the light was at its best. I placed a strawberry pattern covering over the surface to protect it, and put my homemade owl caddy on top along with my old second-hand sewing machine. The drawers were crammed with odd bits of materials; ribbons, buttons, zips, all manner of items that would come in handy, a bit like the popular "everything drawer" most of us possess. It was such a delightful space, so airy and bright, and even just looking at it made me feel like I'd escaped into a new world of oversized chairs and miniature doors and banquets fit for a king.

Hummingbirds and Kaleidoscopes

Now that my sewing space was complete, and I was able to retreat to it once the boys were either in bed or at school and nursery, I was in my element, sewing and putting things together, cutting fabric and teaching myself new skills. When my niece, Eleanor, was two years old, I set to work making her a patchwork quilt for her bed. Up until this point, I'd been concentrating on easier designs, getting the hang of patterns and understanding all the different meanings. So this project was quite challenging back then and definitely the most difficult one I'd faced since I began. It consisted of a series of small squares that I joined together to create a pretty sequence of pink and white, each square containing a different print. The blank squares, which were white, I'd previously sent away to have some words taken from *The Tales of Peter Rabbit* embroidered onto them, and they looked absolutely perfect once stitched alongside the others. In those days, that task would have been a challenge too far for me, but today I wouldn't hesitate. Of course, the fabric and materials I used, along with outsourcing the embroidery work, cost me a small fortune, but it was definitely worth it because little Eleanor loved that quilt just as much as I did.

After finishing that one, I went on to make two more, quite similar, and both were equally as special to me but perhaps for different reasons. One was for my friend's baby, Lottie, who was poorly in hospital. It was a large piece with pink and white squares again, but covered in red roses and flowers and had a ric rac edging in white (a zig zag-designed thin stretch of material, normally used as a trim). The other quilt, or blanket, was a special request for a little girl called Milly, who was also quite unwell. Her mum told me how she needed something to comfort her and my quilts would be the perfect reassurance. More than ten years later, Milly's mum is now a nurse and Milly, now a young woman, still loves and takes comfort from that quilt.

During that time of perfecting my skills making quilts and blankets and learning the intricacies of patchwork designs, I also got a bit obsessed with making Roman blinds. One day the windows would be bare apart from the curtains draped at each end, and the next they would contain a blind; the bay window in the lounge, the kitchen, the bedroom, even the bathroom. I couldn't make them quick enough, but I eventually put that phase behind me, much to Mark's delight, I'm sure, and vowed I'd never make another. I'm glad to say I haven't yet broken that vow!

Our bedroom was starting to resemble a fabric shop as I would go out almost every day buying material and cramming it into drawers and underneath the desk, littering the floor with bits and pieces and trying hard to avoid tripping over any of it. I guess it came to the crunch one day when I realised how untidy the room had become, not wanting my ever-patient husband to think I was literally taking over the whole house. And so I decided to start maintaining some order, declutter and remove the chaos, something that can only be good for the soul in many ways. It was definitely good for mine, and I imagine Mark was feeling happier when he went to bed each night not having to tackle the obstacle course that had overtaken our personal space.

Despite Brady's troubles and the ongoing issues which, at the age of eight, were very much focused on his behavioural needs, he took an interest in sewing himself and asked if he could have a go on my new sewing machine. It had a speed regulator and this made it safer for a beginner to use, so I saw no harm in sitting with him and letting him try it out. I'd never assumed he'd be interested in my hobby so it surprised me, and pleasured me immensely when first asked. Within no time at all, he was cutting out squares and rectangles of fabrics to make cushion covers, the first one which he made for himself. Then one day, he asked if he could make a cover for his friend, Archie, to which I was delighted about. I found him a suitable fabric to use in camouflage and he made a really good job of it, meticulously sewing and stitching and concentrating more than I'd ever known him to. Once he finished that, he went on to make another cushion cover for Aunty Michelle, Mark's sister, who is also Brady's godmother. That one consisted of owls—back to the owl theme—and again, it was beautiful, something she will always treasure, I am sure. Before long, he'd made two more for my mum and Mark's mum. His willingness to learn as I sat next to him was absolutely wonderful to witness, the determination and patience he possessed being such a joy for both Mark and I to see. He listened to me and never faltered in his behaviour, understanding that the sewing machine could be dangerous if not used properly, and he always took my advice on safety very seriously. I was in awe of my boy as he sat at that machine and produced such wonderful creations, and I was incredibly proud of him.

It was in 2015 when I became even braver and started to run a few workshops for keen seamsters in our village hall. People turned up, much to my delight, and perhaps apprehensive back then, and I taught them to make simple items like a reversible bag, Christmas stockings, bunting, and a basic A-line skirt. They would bring their own fabrics and materials and of course a sewing machine, and so long as the machine wasn't too old and had been maintained, was dust free and not in need of a needle change, it was fairly straightforward to show off my skills and help my classes improve their own sewing skills. It was also a nice introduction into teaching and getting a feel for people's needs and demands, something I experienced a lot more of when I would further my career in a couple of years' time. I was teaching mainly skills I'd learned since I'd began sewing as a hobby a few years ago, and it made me realise just how far I'd come. I also knew Brady had helped me to gain the confidence to help others as he'd sit with me for hours wanting to learn, hanging off my every word. He enjoyed being creative and whether he got that from me I don't know, but to feel that my eldest son had enriched my calling to teach others had definitely given me that encouragement I needed to take this hobby to a new level.

In July of that same year I attended a craft show at Doncaster Racecourse and found myself signing up for a workshop called *Make and Take*. It was run by a lady called Jennifer Taylor and I was completely star struck because Jennifer had been a contestant on the very popular TV show *The Great British Sewing Bee*. Such a great person, talented and gentle, and just the right person to be running these workshops. I got chance to chat to her privately and asked her a few questions about her experience on the programme, sharing my own ambitions and dreams to one day do something that would be truly amazing. Something I will never forget her saying to me that day, and I quote it verbatim, was, 'If you want something, don't wait around for a TV show; instead, just make it happen.' It was the best advice I'd received for a very long time, and in such a simple way, too.

It was becoming somewhat overwhelming in our bedroom now, with the amount of boxes and fabric and material constantly scattered about on every available surface, not to mention the desk with my sewing machine on top. Thinking I was making it look tidy, I even hung threads from hooks on the walls, a rainbow of colours that perhaps made our bedroom vibrant and a fun place to be, but some of the threads fell off their hooks and would get tangled and sometimes eaten up by the hoover! Mark, quite understandably, had had enough, and so after a few discussions and conversations about space and the lack of it, we decided I needed somewhere much more practical where I could spread my patterns and the paraphernalia out and not have it clogging up our personal sanctuary. We both wanted our bedroom back and it made sense to get something else sorted.

We had some savings to spare and went searching for a summer house that would fit nicely at the bottom of the garden; nothing too big, but with enough space that I could work comfortably and be able to display my creations without falling over them all the time. My dad helped Mark assemble it and then Mark painted it in a lovely sage green. He put insulation inside and lay carpet tiles on the floor, making it feel warm and cosy.

I acquired an orange tallboy unit to keep my fabric in at one end of the little house, and placed my renovated Alice in Wonderland desk at the other, together with a fabulous orange chair that Mark uplifted for me. In the middle of the house was a table which contained my overlocker. I also put some very personal items in my little house, things that had huge sentimental meaning. One is a plate that Brady splattered with green paint when he was a toddler, together with a vintage sign the boys gave me one Mother's Day. I also had a string of huge, colourful buttons measuring 15cm in diameter in green, yellow and blue, hanging from a hook on the wall. On the same hook was a sign reading *Let's drink tea and talk about lovely things*. That sign now sits on a shelf after I decided to give it its own space.

The space was just enough at the time; it was bright and airy and absolutely perfect, and during the spring and summer months I would throw open the double doors and make it even brighter. I found it so satisfying working on my creations in that little summer house while Mark was sat in the garden just feet away, drinking beer and reading his book. It made me feel close to him, as though we were working together in the same space where we could chat to each other whilst still doing our own thing. He and I have always been so in tune with each other, and he really acknowledges how important sewing is to me, the pleasure it gives and the satisfaction I feel from doing it. He wanted to support this adventure from the beginning, knowing that once I was in my "zone", it would give me the much-needed respite I yearned for.

Of course, come the colder months, particularly those between December and February, I would have to keep those double doors closed to retain the heat and Mark would no longer be sat on the lawn chatting to me while I worked on my latest design. It became a little lonely out there on my own, especially when it was dark outside, and I'd think about my family snuggled inside, radiators on full and watching something on the TV. The kids and Mark did come out to see me occasionally, and I particularly treasured the times when Brady would come into the summer house, usually when I was filming a video for my YouTube channel, as though he was psychic and knew the exact time I'd press *Record*. He always had something to tell me, something he felt was desperately important but perhaps, in my view at any rate, could most definitely have waited until I'd either gone back inside the main house or at least until I'd finished recording! Perhaps, looking back in hindsight, I should have bought myself one of those neon signs to go over the door that they use in a television studio — *On Air* ...

Christmas of 2015, my little summer house was filled with all sorts of crafts I'd made; cushions, note book covers, Christmas stockings, cosmetic bags, hanging hearts, thread catchers, so much crammed into my limited space. Our local church was holding a craft fair in a few days' time and I decided to hire a stall and take some of my creations along, optimistic that I could perhaps shift some of the items, if not all. I was so excited as I spread lots of my things over two tables, taking photos and looking on with such pride. I knew I wouldn't make much money from my sales, that wasn't really why I'd paid the £5 fee for hiring the tables, as I was just so grateful that I'd been able to have this opportunity to sell my wares. Some of the items were really worth quite a lot of money, having used decent fabrics and good quality materials, apart from which, the time that goes into making something can be especially consuming, and so I thought for that alone I'd go home later that day with a bulging cloth bag filled with notes. Unfortunately for me, however, it was a slow day as far as making sales was concerned and all I sold was a gorgeous reverse applique heart-shaped cushion that I'd meticulously made and taken great pride in. I sold the cushion for £12, which meant all I went home with from that Christmas fair was £7. Not exactly sale of the century and definitely nothing to get excited about in the grand scheme of things. But it had been a fun day and I'd chatted to lots of people, so maybe it was worth at least turning up.

In 2016 when I handed my notice in at Acis Group where I'd been working for some time by then, I decided a little respite was in order and took a week off. My new role at Lincoln University as Participation Worker in the School of Health and Social Care was due to begin the following week and I knew I needed to give myself a break, take some time out and prepare myself. It was a role I was really looking forward to and I was determined to make a good impression on my first day. I'd worked hard to achieve that position and to be honest, I really felt I'd earned the job. The interview had been difficult for me as even though I was thrilled to be in with a chance of working in that role, when I walked into the room, I was greeted by two associate professors and the head of the school. It was quite intimidating in some respects and I sat in the chair on the opposite side of the long desk, facing each one and trying to compose myself as I wondered what their questions were going to be. *Where do you see yourself in five years' time?* I guessed was going to be one of them, and though it wasn't, I'm sure I answered it anyway as I tried hard to keep calm and retain the professionalism I needed them to see. I'd made extra effort on my appearance that morning and was pleased with my outfit, and as I was leaving the room after that gruelling hour, one of the professors, the one I'd known for a while, asked if I'd made the dress I was wearing myself. Of course, I had, and I smiled, wondering if she was more interested in my outfit than needing to know if I was the best candidate for the job. But I nodded in response and felt proud when I said, 'Yes, I did.'

I decided during that week off that I would make a mini wardrobe of clothes to wear in my new job, which made the week so enjoyable as I stitched and decided on garments to make. By the end of the week I'd made a knee-length skirt from paisley mini cord, a pussybow blouse from mustard cotton, a purple wood fitted dress with a peplum waist, a pair of fitted trousers, and a cardigan. All in all, it had been a very productive week off!

In early November of that year, I remember commenting on a thread posted on *Sew* magazine's Facebook page about a garment I was currently working on, and I attached a photograph of it to my comment. Amazingly, and much to my surprise, in *Sew's* November edition, they featured my comment as their "Star Letter" and wrote a lovely comment underneath saying, *What a beautiful idea, Lucy. Free motion embroidery is such a fun way of creating stitch drawings that are also totally unique.* I was thrilled to see they'd appreciated my work. In January 2017, I decided to make a more ambitious item, a lap quilt by piecing bits of fabric together to create a sequence of houses. On top of each house I applied some free motion embroidery stitching and applique to personalise each one. On one of them, I embroidered a little coupe car that my boys loved to play in on summer days, and a washing line with miniature pants and bras hung onto it. It was a small creation, but I was immensely proud of it and at the end of that month whilst sat watching my favourite sewing programme one Sunday morning, I sent a message to the channel telling them about the quilt and giving some details about it, along with a photo, and to my absolute surprise they showed it on air. To say that made my day was an understatement!

It's safe to say that by now, my confidence had grown considerably and this was becoming so much more than a hobby. My little summer house was quickly filling up with anything and everything and I'd spend so much time putting things away and keeping things in order. I guess some people call it OCD, and really, I'm not sure what I'd call it. But the truth of the matter is that I get quite anxious when things become messy, unruly, and I often find myself feeling out of control and unable to function properly. Having two young boys to look after as well as everything else I was juggling with was, as you can imagine, putting a strain on my mental health, and even though I wouldn't have wanted to be anywhere else than in my sewing utopia or with my beautiful family, I knew that eventually I'd need to address what was staring me in the face: chaos. It first came to light years previously when Brady was a baby and I found myself obsessively cleaning the house, which I felt needed doing, but which raised a few eyebrows when people discovered I was hoovering ceilings on a daily basis. Because it was seen as something unusual, I received a few sessions of therapy to try and get to the bottom of why I was doing it, and it was concluded that I could have been suffering with post-natal depression, and the constant cleaning was my way of coping.

But my increasing confidence over the last few years made me feel sure about purchasing my first Merchant and Mills Pattern, The Factory Dress. The pattern and sheets of instructions, packaged in beautiful white, heavy duty wrapping paper, was something else, and I went out to a store in Lincoln called Fabric Corner, which is now my favourite source of fabrics. The dress had a drape that held its shape when it came to turning through the collar pieces; it also had a pocket on the chest, turned back sleeve cuffs, pockets and tucks to the front and back, and its design print was made up of the tiniest black and white checks. It looked incredible on a hanger. I wanted it to look incredible on me too, but my petite frame perhaps wasn't doing it justice and I reckon I only wore it a few times in the end.

My dad benefitted in May of that year when I made him a fabulous pair of very smart pyjamas in pale blue with red stitching and a dark blue stitching to the pockets. I bound every seam with claret satin binding and Dad was super proud when I gave them to him. He tried them on and they fit him perfectly. Homemade presents are always the best, in my opinion. Amongst all these sewing projects that were only adding to my confidence, I was still very much carrying out my motherly duties, finding letters in school bags and making the usual mad last minute dash to throw costumes together—Batman capes for Haydn and a hedgehog outfit for Brady's nativity play... *Don't ask!*

Chapter Five

I remember being at the top of the abseiling tower, all harnessed up. It felt like I was fifty metres up in the air but I bet it was no more than twenty, in all honesty. 'Lean back,' the instructor said, 'just hold the ropes and gently lean back into the air, and let the ropes do all the work.' I was terrified, but I really wanted to do this. Slowly and steadily down the side of the tower I went and as I neared the ground, I felt like I wanted to burst with excitement because I'd done it ...
"Blackwell Bag"

Some children find starting school a daunting prospect whilst others embrace it and you wonder how they managed without it for the last four or five years. Haydn, with his cuteness and tiny frame, spiky hair that he insisted was going to be his style, was of the former variety of children and it could be quite difficult at times having to persuade him how exciting school could be. Little grey shorts, a pale-blue collared T-shirt, and a navy V-neck sweater made up his uniform, but he hated that sweater and it was often a battle to get him to keep it on.

He didn't like primary school and his first year there was utterly miserable for him. It was such a wrench having to dry his tears before we'd set off, and I'd be fighting to keep my own tears at bay, feeling guilty for sending my little boy out into the big wide world when all he really wanted to do was either stay with me, or spend the day with Vanessa, his childminder—he called her *Banessa*. He'd been looked after by Vanessa since he was ten months old, and this new phase in his life, a whole different journey than the one he'd been used to for most of his short life, was just too much for him.

He'd got into a routine that he enjoyed and like many other children his age whose parents work, it was hard for him to adapt and understand that he had no choice but to go to school now. His days of being cared for in someone else's house, being able to play and snack and talk when he wanted to, had unfortunately for him come to end, but to expect a four-year-old child to acknowledge that, was going to be a challenge in anyone's world.

School, of course, is much more structured and children are encouraged to do so much more than play in sandpits or run around outside. Haydn wanted to be a free spirit; he wanted to use his imagination as he played with his beloved trains, and not have to go back to the classroom when the teacher shouted for everyone to go inside. We were told often when we'd pick him up during that first year in primary school that he was unwilling to sit at a desk and wasn't engaging how he should be, instead seeming desperate to go outside and play, run off steam. At that first parents' evening his teacher said he would have benefitted from another year at nursery, but obviously that would never have been possible. We needed Haydn to start growing up now, learn to adjust and feel comfortable with a different routine and a new set of rules. But it was becoming obvious that he was perhaps a year or two behind in educational terms, though his social skills were, in our opinion, perfectly fine.

We had to work to Haydn's timeframe and hope that he would eventually catch up with his peers, but over the next year, it was obvious that his reading and writing skills were poor and he needed extra support to get him through. We knew he'd been upset on the occasions when Brady's meltdowns hit, and we were fully aware that this could have an impact on him, but he was still unhappy at school and we had to reach the conclusion that what was going on with his brother was most definitely affecting him.

One of Haydn's favourite activities was the weekly swimming lesson with school. A double decker bus would pull up at the gates and all the kids from the school would pile on, bags filled with swimming costumes and towels thrown over shoulders or hanging from little hands as they found a seat. It was this day that he didn't mind getting up for school or putting his sweater on, and he would actually smile as we'd leave the house. For an hour or so during that day, he wouldn't be tethered to a desk or having to listen to a teacher at the front of the class, and would instead be learning how to swim, something he loved so much more than traditional school work.

I remember on one of his swimming days he came home with his wet trunks and damp towel, and as usual handed me the bag to get everything dried again. I made tea and we all sat at the table, and he seemed a bit glum, which was unusual on a day he'd been to the leisure centre. 'The teachers are mean,' he suddenly blurted out whilst tucking into chicken nuggets and chips. I looked at Mark and shrugged. We'd never heard him say that before and we were quite sure none of the teachers were indeed mean. So we asked him what he meant by that and he repeated himself, this time adding that they had made him cry.

I put down my knife and fork and leaned over towards him, holding his little hand in mine as I asked him to explain what he meant. We were obviously quite confused, and both a little worried about this admission, as we'd never seen anything to give us cause for alarm. 'Take your time,' I said to him. 'Just tell us what's happened.'

He pushed another chicken nugget into his mouth and chewed it impatiently, while Mark and I watched him, now feeling a bit perturbed and perhaps secretly wondering if we'd need to go into school and have a chat with the headmistress.

'When we go swimming,' he began, 'we get dried after we've been in the pool and get dressed, then we all wait in the reception to get on the bus.' Mark and I nodded, imagining a load of kids hanging around, hair wet, tired and eager to get back, probably excited and making a raucous din in the entrance of the leisure centre, teachers doing a head count and having to repeat it because a couple of kids were still lingering about in the changing rooms trying in vain to tie shoe laces. It was a familiar image, and we were still confused and now quite eager to hear what our little boy was going to reveal.

'Well,' he continued, 'every week we have to walk past the chocolate machine but the teachers never buy us anything. They just tell us to hurry up and get on the bus.' He was referring to the vending machine that would often eat our money in return for a bar of chocolate or a packet of crisps after we'd taken the boys swimming ourselves. I looked at Mark, who had now also put his knife and fork down, and we both burst out laughing. Bless our sweet boy; how innocent and cute. But I guess, through a child's eyes, that is pretty mean!

When Brady started secondary school in September 2016, we decided that it would be beneficial for Haydn to change schools to the local newbuild primary, and to put him in a much smaller environment with fewer pupils in each class. He needed more one-to-one learning and to catch up with his reading and writing, so when Mark and I took him to have a look around, we had the job of assessing it for ourselves and making sure it would be the right move. The last thing we wanted to do was to keep disrupting Haydn's education, especially as things hadn't gone great for Brady either in those early years. The teachers there were more than happy to welcome us and we sat in the headmaster's office for a chat about our son's needs and explained our concerns about his slow progress. I suggested that he start in the next term, which would have been after Christmas, but the headmaster shook his head and politely disagreed, saying he felt Haydn should be enrolled as soon as possible because he had every confidence he would have him reading by the time they broke up for the Christmas holidays.

We felt confident about what he'd said and liked his approach to Haydn's needs, and within five days of that meeting, our youngest child started at that new school. His whole demeanour changed. He was a happy child again, full of life and looking forward to going to school.

He enjoyed his days there and had fun with his peers, making new friends quickly and engaging well with the teachers. We noticed progress in his reading within two weeks of him being there and it was an absolute joy to see him eager to pick up a book and slide his finger along the words whilst he read them to us, slowly, but surely.

Perhaps it was the ethos of the school, the style of teaching, the characteristics of the staff, but whatever it was that seemed so different to his first primary school, we knew without a doubt that we'd done the right thing in moving him. We were so proud of him and what he was starting to achieve.

Mark would drop Haydn off at school in the morning on his way to work and either he or I would collect him at home time. But once the warmer weather approached, Mark would more often than not walk him to school as it wasn't far, and it gave him the exercise, of course, too. Both Haydn and Mark enjoyed those walks—quality father and son time, where Haydn would fill his dad in on the events of the day. Haydn's always been somewhat of a chatterbox and would bend Mark's ear with all the excitement of playtime and lunch breaks and what he'd been learning in the classroom. I'd go with him some afternoons if I was at home, and we'd find ourselves standing in the queue for the ice cream van that was always parked at the top of the slope a few yards from the school. Haydn's eyes would light up as the man handed his "Birdsnest" ice cream to him—a swirl of ice-creamy goodness with bubble-gum and sprinkles on the top! And even though he went swimming with his new school, to a different leisure centre situated next door, he didn't complain any more about teachers not buying him anything from the "chocolate machine".

Chapter Six

It was 2005. The sun was shining brightly and the flowers were in full bloom in our little back garden in Wintern Court. Mark has always been a keen gardener, making sure the weeds are kept at bay and the flowers burst with all the colours of the rainbow in every corner of the garden. I decided to serve tea in the garden that day. The parasol was up and the table was laid ready for a delicious salad. But food wasn't really what this was all about. I poured us both a glass of wine and asked if I could make a toast. Mark smiled and raised his glass as I raised both our spirits and announced,
'I'm pregnant.' ...
"Wintern Basket Collection"

It was Wednesday, 20th September 2017, when things came to a head and I decided to start writing almost-daily entries into a journal. I asked myself the question over and over again, *Is it okay to not be okay?* and couldn't find any answers that would offer me reassurance. Brady was just eleven years old and now at secondary school, somewhere that was still so new to him. He was reaching that difficult age of hormones and trying desperately to make sense of the world around him, while Mark and I were desperate to understand the world in which we were now living. Brady used the school bus to get to and from school and after only a few weeks of him starting there, one afternoon he failed to come home after being dropped off at his usual stop on the main road. Like all school children in these days of mobile phones, we'd bought him one and allowed him to take it to school, mainly for emergencies, phone calls, texts, etc. When I rang him after realising he was late, the ring tone continued emitting in my ear until it went to voicemail. I tried a few more times until it was becoming obvious he wasn't going to pick up. So I left the house on foot and walked through the estate towards the main road hoping to find him skulking somewhere, maybe coming out of a shop with a bag of crisps and a can of pop. But I didn't find him and naturally I began to worry, making my way back home just as Mark arrived in the drive. He then drove around and eventually found our son at the local park, seeming not to care and nonchalantly getting in the car when Mark ordered him to.

I explained to him how worried we'd been and that if he was going to be late home it was always important to let us know; the fact he had a mobile phone for such purposes meant he could always keep those lines of communication open. But it was as though he genuinely didn't care that we were worried. I wasn't even sure he was listening to me as I voiced my concerns and tried to reason with him, and his response was to tell me to stop moaning at him as he stomped up to his bedroom. I'd never wanted to smother either of my boys and because of Brady's difficulties, I tended to take a step back and allow him the space to at least try and understand what being part of a loving family actually meant. But after we'd eaten dinner that evening, he went back out, announcing he was going to the park to play. Much to my annoyance, he didn't take his phone, which meant if he didn't come home when he was supposed to, I'd end up worrying again and no doubt need to talk to him yet again about how unfair he was being.

The time came when he should have been getting home and as I feared, he didn't return. Mark once more got in the car and went out in search, his first port of call of course being the park, where Brady had told us he would be. But he wasn't at the park. He'd wandered off elsewhere and when Mark did finally bring him home, stressed and annoyed at having to go looking for him for the second time that day, I can honestly say that my eldest son became someone else that night. He wailed at us and shouted obscenities, hitting his fists against walls; it was all quite disturbing to watch. We tried hard to calm him down, me with a cup of tea and Mark with his calming words, but Brady was having none of it, and the fact that Haydn was hearing and witnessing his older brother's meltdown was upsetting me immensely. Haydn was just five years old, and I'd already started wondering how much Brady's behaviour would affect him, though Haydn was a calm child and tended to stay out of the way when the meltdowns began.

But as the days went on, things got progressively worse in our household as the stress and tension in the atmosphere became almost unbearable. I got to the point where I wasn't looking forward to my boy coming home from school, frightened of the mood he might be in, worrying that he would be angry again or have another meltdown. At the same time, I was terrified he wouldn't come home at all and we'd end up losing him. On the

Wednesday of the following week, 27th September, Brady again failed to come home and so I made my way to the bus stop on the main road, once more hoping to see him and hoping I could somehow coax him to come back. But he was nowhere to be found, and it was 5pm when he finally came through the front door as though it was perfectly okay that he had arrived home more than an hour later than he was expected to. I tried to reason with him again, explaining how wrong it was not to let me know where he was, but as if on repeat, he wasn't listening and just started shouting at me. Mark and I had told him the previous night that he wouldn't be able to go to the park for a while, at least until he'd thought about his unruly behaviour and how much stress it was causing, but after dinner, he asked if he could go, perhaps knowing underneath what the answer was going to be. He was a boy, growing up and discovering himself, wanting to play and appear like one of the lads. I didn't blame him for asking really, but when I sent him back upstairs to do his homework, English in particular that was due in the following day, he reluctantly sauntered to his bedroom and rushed through it, his focus obviously being on the sooner he finished, the sooner he could leave the house and go to the park.

We refused him when he came back down and he spent the next hour and a half literally screaming and shouting at us and probably giving the neighbours cause for concern too, never mind us. Poor Haydn was distraught and my worry for him escalated to almost breaking point that night. But Mark, also, was in bits as he sat on the stairs, his head in his hands as Brady ran through the front door, slamming it behind him. 'Why won't anyone help us?' Mark said, and it was a question I absolutely could not answer.

Brady came back home eventually, a bit calmer though still angry and shouting, and while he'd been out, I'd rung my mum to tell her what was happening. She came over just as he arrived, and managed to calm him down, seeing how upset Mark and I were and also worrying about Haydn and the effect this was having on him. Mum took Brady back to her house for the night and our house was once more silent. We all needed some space, and we made sure Brady understood that staying at his nanny's wasn't a punishment but was just a change of scenery for him away from me and his dad. The next morning when I got up, I had a long shower, standing under the jets as the hot water cascaded over me, my eyes closed and thoughts racing through my head. What were we dealing with here? Where was all this heading? I had never been so frightened in my life as I was then. Not knowing what was around the corner was the most daunting prospect to ever enter my mind.

I am a punch bag, and because I'm his mum, I must accept that abuse.

That's what I wrote in my journal on Thursday, 28th September. Some parents wouldn't agree with that statement, but I was always so determined to do everything I possibly could to give both my boys the best upbringing they deserved. Brady's conditions were crippling us all, but it wasn't his fault he was like this. Mark and I had nurtured him and supported him and stood by his side through thick and thin, going through the disappointments with his education since and witnessing how hard it had been for him to fit in anywhere. We were good parents, and still are, and that is something that will never change. So many applications had been put forward for us to receive help, not just for Brady but for our family as a whole. We needed a break—both from the mental torment as well as the lack of support from the local authority. When he was yet again refused help from Children's Services, we were not only frustrated now but angry, too. Our boy needed help. We needed help. Haydn needed help to cope with all this chaos, yet none was forthcoming and for what felt like the hundredth time, we had to accept that we were on our own.

That night, when Brady refused to come home from the park again, Mark went to collect him and ordered him to get in the car. The abuse we both received from our eleven-year-old when he came through the door was beyond unacceptable. His language alone was upsetting as he lashed out at us verbally, calling us names and using horrendously vulgar words. Storming up to his room and slamming the door, all we heard was screaming and shouting coming from within and then the sound of scraping, which we later learned was Brady making dents and causing damage to his bedroom walls. Mark was utterly distraught at this point and even told Brady he would have to leave if this abuse continued. The shouting didn't stop and Mark was really struggling to hold it together. I managed to coax him downstairs and keep them apart after Mark realised he was getting nowhere, but of course Haydn was in the house and once things seemed to be calming down a little, my poor little boy came into the lounge and sat on the sofa with us and said, 'Brady can hit me if he needs to.'

We were heartbroken. This was just too sad for words. My boys are my world, along with Mark, of course, and no matter how much I love them both equally, I absolutely hated this situation with a passion.

The next day, I received a phone call from Miss Brace at Brady's school telling me they had issued a warning letter for bad behaviour, which Brady had undertaken on the school bus. I guess it was a call I'd been waiting for, though had obviously hoped to avoid, but there she was, Miss Brace being reasonable and listening to me as I explained our current situation and how impossible it had become. We were at a loss as to what to do or where to go from here, and Miss Brace came to our rescue by holding the meeting that would lead to the Early Help referral. She advised me to start a dialogue with Brady about how we could work towards fixing the mess that had been brewing, probably for some time.

We decided it was best all round that Brady stayed with my mum for a couple of nights that weekend. He seemed to enjoy being with my mum and it gave all of us the much-needed respite. When the postman arrived the following week, I could have kissed him when he handed over a letter with the NHS logo, telling us that Brady had been accepted for a community paediatric assessment. There was a waiting list of eighteen weeks, but the fact we were finally being taken seriously was something to celebrate. That letter also stated that, in the meantime, the school would initiate Early Help to ensure that all our needs, Brady's and the family's, were being met. Miss Brace was a legend to me then.

She had listened and understood and knew how much we needed help. Her experience and knowledge in the education system was second to none. We were now parents of a child with special needs who were at last being recognised as people desperate for expert support.

After the recent turmoil and unbelievably difficult days we'd all endured as a family, the entries that followed in my journal were so much more pleasurable to document. Whether it was the idea of us being taken seriously and now knowing that help was on its way, or perhaps the warning that Brady had received concerning his bad behaviour on the bus, I can't be sure, but things seemed to settle down somewhat and with minimal fuss, we actually enjoyed our time together. We took the boys swimming and shopping, where Brady got new shoes, and then went into the pet shop where the boys fussed over the small animals. The assistant in the shop was so impressed with how Brady had conducted himself that he commented to Mark and I how good our eldest son was around the animals; knowledgeable and well-mannered, even saying that if he wanted to work in the shop when he turned fifteen, he would consider it. I left that shop with a spring in my step and a huge grin that would have lit up the whole of Lincolnshire!

That following week was the dreaded parents' evening, perhaps not a dread so much for us, but usually for the poor kids who get anxious about what will be said about them by teachers they're supposed to look up to. But much to our surprise and absolute joy, it turned out that Brady was making a vast improvement and was doing extremely well. His teachers were happy with him, telling us he was above average in most subjects, getting A's and B's in tests. We all came away happy that night and I noticed Brady had a sparkle in his eyes as we left the school and got in the car. We got home and all sat in the lounge, together, as a family should. There was no arguing or bickering or shouting or abuse. Just Mark, my beautiful boys, and me, watching the TV and dipping into bags of crisps and drinking pop. If anyone had been looking through our bay window, they would have seen the perfect nuclear family: Mum, Dad, Brady and Haydn, not forgetting the cats, of course.

However, perfection never lasts and our amazing week of calm, peace and tranquillity, unfortunately came to an abrupt end during the last week of October when Brady's first appointment with Peter Ludlow, Consultant Clinical Psychologist who specialised in autism (now retired), was upon us. Before we were due to set off, Brady ran away and when he eventually came back, he went into one of the worst meltdowns we'd seen to date. I rang my parents, asking them to come over and see if they could calm him, but he was too far gone by that point and stood in the street screaming and shouting at us, hurling the usual bad language and abuse. We managed to get him into the car eventually, but he continued his tirade of lashing out obscenities and scaring us so much that in the end one of us called the police, though I can't recall which one of us that was. An officer in uniform attended our house and talked to Brady, along with the rest of us, which managed to simmer down the situation. We did attend the appointment in the end, albeit an hour late, where we learned that his emotional intelligence is below his actual age, something that didn't come as a shock to us,

I admit. But that appointment gave us some answers to the burning questions we so desperately needed answering, and another appointment was made for us the following week.

Once again, things calmed down a little and we went on to enjoy a pleasant few days, and even though his behaviour at school was often unacceptable, he seemed to enjoy the detentions he was dished out at least once a week. Takes all sorts, I guess!

One good thing that happened during that time was for Brady to introduce us to some of his friends, the ones he'd started to hang out with at the park. He brought a few of them back one afternoon and even though we needed to set a few boundaries, they were good kids and enjoyed being in our house. I loved to see that sparkle return to Brady's eyes when he brought his friends home, as though proud of where we live, and I'd like to think proud of his parents, too. One of the most wonderful traits he possesses is his loyalty to his friends, and that has never changed. Something he wrote for me during this time, though I can't remember exactly when, consists of one sentence written in red pen on a sheet of A4 paper, and that will stay with me to my grave:

> *If I had a wish, one last wish, I would spend it on you.*

Our next appointment with Peter was lengthy—three hours in total—and Mark had a streaming cold and could have really done without it. We talked through so much going all the way back to when Brady was born and the traits he developed from a very young age.

'The signs were there,' Peter told us, as we explained his behaviour even back then. And I felt somewhat relieved to know it wasn't my fault that our dear boy had these complex conditions; I wasn't a bad parent and neither was Mark. Brady was simply "different" in some ways, and his needs were more complicated than that of other children not on the autism spectrum. It was Peter who finally gave us the official diagnosis that made us realise there was no need to be scared anymore. The unknown was still very much at the forefront of our minds, but we were gaining some control of the situation, we were able to learn more about how we could help Brady and how we, as a family, could move forward.

No two children are the same, and when I hear other parents or adults commenting on a child being "naughty" because he or she can't control their behaviour, not knowing the full facts, it can be extremely frustrating. We have always done our best as parents, always reached out for help, and it was only then that we had been able to say for definite that our boy wasn't being difficult or argumentative on purpose, he was simply searching for meaningful answers and trying to understand this world around him that would have seemed so alien to his young mind. He's a clever boy, the staff had confirmed that to us in parents' evening, and I'd seen him concentrating so hard when I'd taught him how to use the sewing machine; the determination on his face and the way he listened to my instructions. He wanted to learn and though it was often a challenge for him to fully absorb what he was being taught, it didn't stop him being eager to do well in his education.

At our final meeting with Peter in December, another

lengthy sit-down session when fortunately Mark was no longer full of a cold, it was explained to us how complex Brady's condition really was and Peter was able to spend time helping us to understand the chemistry and biology of our son's brain. Things really started to make sense as we learned how one part of his brain is pretty much asleep, preventing him from having inhibitions, thus causing him to say things he perhaps wouldn't mean to say normally. He's disorganised emotionally and this means he requires a lot of patience not to mention spoon feeding if something needs to be done. His mind is less connected than that of his frontal lobe and this makes him anxious, constantly looking for and checking for anything that could worry him or be cause for concern. When he's anxious, he then goes into fight or flight mode, which means he either argues or goes into a low state of mind, and when that anxiety is at its highest, he can suffer with amnesia where he has no recollection of the event that took place. It was incredibly interesting to learn all this, but it was exhausting at the same time, for both Mark and I. But we knew, as his parents, it would have been ten-times more exhausting for Brady.

While all this was going on, we also had to consider Haydn, not just because of what he kept witnessing with his brother, but because he seemed to have a problem with his hearing, and in the end we made the decision to move him to a different school. The headmistress of his previous school wasn't understanding our concerns or Haydn's lack of communication. By the beginning of December, he had been put on the waiting list to see a specialist within the ENT department at hospital and I was very hopeful that his issues would be easily rectified and he would start to excel in his new school. I was genuinely excited about the move because after extensive research, we'd learned that the academy was well equipped to deal with the support he would need.

It had been a difficult time for us as a family, having to deal with all the extra worries that often come with having children, but I felt as though the good days were starting to overtake the bad ones. We had a way forward and a plan set in place, a diagnosis and some support, yet the next few months proved just as hard when Brady started to experience night-time anxiety, waking in the night, terrified. Mark and I took it in turns to watch over him, leaving lamps and lights on throughout the house and even positioning his teddies in a kind of formation that looked a little like an advancing army. We just wanted him to feel safe and this was our way of helping our boy. But his struggles were getting worse and we went to the chemist one day to see if they could suggest anything to help him sleep. They did: Phenergan, also known as Promethazine. These worked and he slept in till 11am on his birthday, which was totally unheard of. It wasn't to be a long term solution, of course, but we agreed that he could take it again the following night, just to help him function a little better if nothing else.

We made an appointment with the GP, who was very helpful, and assisted us by chasing up the referral to Community Paediatrics with the view that Melatonin, a drug commonly used for people with ADHD, would be beneficial to him at this stage. There was a waiting list, as always, and we were told it was okay to let him take the Phenergan occasionally in the meantime.

For his twelve birthday, we organised a trip to the local sports centre for Brady and his friends to go wall climbing and play football, and it was quite disheartening to see that he wasn't really excited about it. We knew this was normal for him, but when only two of the children we'd invited turned up out of about six, I have to admit it made me quite annoyed. We knew our boy perhaps wasn't the easiest kid to make friends with, but he was loyal to his friends and he'd brought them back to the house now several times. His words brought tears to my eyes when he said some years later, 'They disappointed me, Mum, but they didn't like me.' I always felt it was more a reflection on them than it was on Brady and I felt so very sad for him that day. He'd even made his own birthday cake in the shape of a castle and I was incredibly proud of him. His two friends looked at it in awe and I think we were all a little apprehensive about cutting into it because it was such a work of art!

We go through so much as parents, taking all our children's woes on as though they're ours, too. I've only ever wanted my sons to be happy and I know they are, in their own way, of course. Giving them both the independence we feel they need as well as always being there for them when they need to talk or just need a cuddle has always been, and always will be, paramount in our family unit, and no matter what struggles lie ahead, that will never change.

Chapter Seven

The alarms went off at 2am, telling us it was time to get up and get ready for the long trip up north to Skipsea. The caravan was hooked up to the van, which was packed with all the essentials. A blow-up bed had been inflated and was on the floor next to the three-seater bench in the back of the van. Me and the twins would travel in the back whilst my little brother sat in the front with our parents. The idea was that we could sleep in the bed on the long journey up, but the reality was that we rolled around on the floor and bounced about as the wheels turned along the bumpy roads ...
"Skirlington"

Haydn went on to enjoy his primary school after we'd moved him in 2016, and by the time he finished he'd made some very good friends, ones I'm sure he'll be in contact with for years to come. I took a lovely photograph of him and three of his friends at their leavers' assembly, all with their arms around each other, and I had to smile at my boy who was still head and shoulders shorter than his peers. He was starting to develop his own character and along with his overgrown, floppy fringe, his identity was coming into its own with his new love for Anime and books; lots and lots of books!

He was adamant not to attend the same secondary school as Brady, and instead wanted to go to the local secondary school just five minutes' walk from our house. I wasn't sure about this and Mark and I spent some time discussing what was best. But whilst rearing our boys, we've always preferred to be guided by their decisions rather than push our decisions onto them and one day maybe suffer the consequences of their resentment. So, after a long chat and realising that Haydn was quite sure about his choice of secondary school, we got him a place there and hoped it would all work out for the best.

Unfortunately for Haydn, however, it wasn't long into the new term when he started coming home with bruises on his body and Mark and I knew only too well that because our boy was quite shy, he was probably being pushed around. We noticed a shift in his moods and he became quiet and somewhat withdrawn, uncomfortable about answering our questions and talking to us about what was going on. He was mixing with the "big boys" now, and like many children who go from a fairly enclosed environment like primary school can be, to a school where the kids are much bigger and stronger, and of course much older, it was definitely causing him a few problems. Our loud, vivacious, youngest son with so much life and a thirst for adventure had become quiet and shy, and naturally, it was upsetting to see.

One Friday evening, I was in the lounge and Haydn, I thought, was in his room drawing. Suddenly, his little face appeared round the door and he hovered as if wondering whether to come in or not. There was clearly something bothering him and I'd been patient up to now, waiting for him to make the first move and tell me what it was. I moved up on the sofa and he sat next to me, then he said, 'Mum, if I hadn't gone to my new secondary school, which one would I have gone to?' This told me straight away that he wasn't sure about the decision he'd made to attend the school nearest to home. We talked for some time that night, probably a few hours, and he opened up to me about how miserable he was at secondary school and that he was being picked on. As his parents, we'd known something was wrong and so I got straight on to Brady's school the following Monday morning by sending an email to the headmaster, asking if there might be a place there for Haydn. We were invited in the following week to have a look around and decided there and then to move him. The transition was done efficiently and it wasn't long before he started at his new school. He adapted really quickly, which was such a relief, and even got used to the travelling, which meant a much longer day for him from start to finish. We saw a difference in him within weeks as he came home smiling, seemingly happy and looking forward to going back the following day. So much different to how he'd been previously.

His progress, even though appearing to be on the up, was still slower than it should have been and we decided to start investigating why that could be. With Brady having special needs, we knew the procedure and where we'd need to start the ball rolling, and after appointments and assessments and the usual question and answer sessions, it was concluded that Haydn has two conditions known as Dyscalculia, which is associated with numbers and maths, appertaining to a person being unable to make sense of calculations, and the other condition is Dysgraphia, a disability that prevents a person reading and writing to their age-appropriate level. This explained so much of what had been going on with him throughout primary school. He'd struggled to learn in these key subjects of Maths and English, and now we knew why.

Something he was exceptionally good at, however, was, and still very much is, art and anything creative. We could see this from an early age as he'd sit for hours drawing and painting and colouring in. It pleased me immensely to see him take after me in this way, especially when Brady was also keen to learn how to sew. He started drawing incredible illustrations that left me in awe of his talent, and one of the things he became obsessed at drawing was Anime, the Japanese doll-like figures, many with floppy fringes like his. I really started to encourage him, telling him how good these drawings were, mainly because they were, but also because, like me, he sometimes lacks confidence and needed to hear it. I bought him painting sets and expensive colouring pens and his skills improved as he'd sit at the table or in his room for hours just filling in sketchbook after sketchbook with an imagination that simply blew my mind. I started taking him to creative pottery shops where we'd sit down at a large table and find something to paint, and he'd just lap it up. Something we still do together now.

Star Wars characters, Japanese characters, trains and a fabulous drawing of Thomas the Tank Engine all materialised in his sketchbooks, and he would tear each page out and thrust it at me for my approval. It was a constant *Wow* from me!

Even though Haydn suffers from Dysgraphia, he has a huge love for Anime books, and these are read backwards. He'd been slow at developing his reading skills, but there he was, shelves full of these unusual books that he sits and reads over and over again. It's something I'll always buy for him because it's brought him on leaps and bounds and shown us that he's a very talented young man. He also sings Japanese songs, his deep fascination for Japan knowing no bounds, and he has ambitions to live there one day. A lot of his clothes have Anime characters on them, which just adds to his obsession of posters that adorn every wall in his bedroom. He has a loyal friendship circle also, all of whom love anything Anime.

Perhaps because of his difficulties where writing is concerned, he's particularly good at describing something in words, explaining in great detail what he's thinking, as if reading it out loud from a book. If you asked Brady what colour the sky is, he will answer with his literal mind—it's either blue, grey, or black. Whereas Haydn will describe the sky in all its finery, the clouds, their shape, different colours, any contrails from passing aircraft. He'll also tell you what it reminds him of, something he might have seen on TV recently, or a picture he's seen somewhere, maybe something that happened when he was younger. His imagination is inspiring.

He also has a love for trains and when he was three, after he'd been quite poorly with Strep Throat, we took both boys to Kent where we stayed in my friend's dad's flat in the seaside town of Broadstairs. We spent some wonderful days on the beaches and Haydn would play happily on the sand with his trains, burying them and building around them. We took him to a toy shop on one of our many trips to that beautiful town, and gave both boys some money to spend. Haydn went straight to the shelf containing various trains and chose one called "Ashima" from the Thomas the Tank Engine range. He described it as 'The most beautifullest train there ever was' and he absolutely treasured her, holding her carefully in his hands and trying desperately to protect her. But within just thirty minutes of leaving the shop, he dropped her in the sea and she was lost forever.

We couldn't bear seeing how upset he was, screaming and crying and completely distraught. And so, an hour later, we traipsed back to that toy shop and bought him another Ashima, which he's kept safe from harm ever since!

Broadstairs is quite near the Hornby museum, so we always made a point of visiting two or three times each time we visited the area. Mark has taken him to several railway museums. Trains give him comfort and even though we've been a little concerned about the fact he's never grown out of his love for Thomas the Tank Engine and Friends, we know that, just like Spiderman and Doctor Who gives Brady peace of mind when he's anxious, Haydn's love for trains lessens his own stress, too.

Chapter Eight

Mum and Dad moved into their first family home in 1975 when they were given a new-build three-bedroomed council house in Exham Close. It was part of the Woodloes Park residential development on four hundred hectares of farmland. They went on to buy that house in 1979 under the Right-to-Buy scheme. At that time, Woodloes Park was still developing and as children, we would play in the park by the Grand Union Canal and walk up the hill to what was known to the locals as "Devil's Rock". It was rumoured to be haunted and feared by most ...
"Woodloes"

My summer house-cum-sewing room was starting to become extremely crowded and it was obvious to both Mark and I that I needed more space. Things were moving on and my magpie characteristics of buying everything that caught my eye to use for sewing garments and other items, was really prominent as it got increasingly more chaotic with drawers, cupboards and shelves full to bursting. I could feel myself getting stressed on a regular basis and started to feel somewhat boxed in with too little free space around me. My need to be in control has always been one of my traits, which is perhaps why it hit me so hard to learn about Brady's condition—something I was most definitely *not* in control of. You could probably say it's both a strength and a curse that affects me in equal measure.

We have a single garage that we used partly for the treadmill and partly to store the usual outdoor items; bikes, gardening tools, household maintenance stuff, etc. And so it was decided that we would convert the garage and turn it into a workshop for me, leaving a big enough space at one end for the things we had no room for in the house. It was a great idea and my dad and Mark set about on the conversion, dropping beams onto the floor, insulating the walls and adding a suspended ceiling. It didn't take long to do and we soon started to move all my equipment in, meaning the summer house would become a slightly different style of sanctuary, with a cosy sofa, a bookcase and a table, decorated with most of the same items I'd already got in there—Brady's paint-splattered plate, the oversized colourful buttons, a shelf containing books, and some plants dotted about.

The garage, on the other hand, was now my new studio and even though it was a little dark at first, it was absolutely wonderful to have a much bigger space and a lot more room to put things away. The large table was perfect for laying out fabric and cutting out, patterns were displayed on shelves underneath, and I stacked materials on shelves along the walls. There was plenty space to set up my two sewing machines and the overlocker, and I displayed my rainbow of threads on a stand affixed to the wall.

Like most other people in these days of technology, I'd been using social media for several years by now, Facebook in particular, and along with my own personal page where I posted photos and talked more about family matters, I did try to give my sewing a mention but didn't feel it was being acknowledged so much by the friends I had on there. So I decided to set up a hobby page in 2015 and called it *Sew Pretty*. There, I talked about my creations and posted photos and generated a lot more interest from like-minded people who were also keen to read about anything sewing related. I found it to be a huge success and so I went on to have custom designed labels printed so I could stitch them on the designs I made. I got such a buzz out of seeing my own branded label on clothes, displaying them with pride on my page. I kept contemplating that name, but was limited to what I could name the page on Facebook. However, in 2018, I came up with the new name of *Sew Pretty Sew Mindful*, which I knew was much more relevant to what I was about.

The whole concept felt so professional, and I was hugely proud of what I'd achieved. I was getting requests from people wanting to look at the studio and see for themselves how we'd converted it, look at the space I now had to improve my sewing skills and get even more creative. Of course, now, as this book is being written, my social media presence has increased ten-fold and I have a large following on Instagram, too, who I'm pleased to say join in with my "live" events and videos, chatting to me as I beaver away in the studio. I remember the first post I ever shared on Instagram was a photo of me wearing a dress called *Helena* by *Sew Me Something*—pale blue and white linen fabric. It had pintucks down the centre front, full facing neckline, sleeves with button plackets, and inset pockets.

Hummingbirds and Kaleidoscopes

Social media has been a godsend to me over the years, as well as the internet and the way we can just search for something—a shop, a place, reviews, etc. Being an avid user of online forums and groups, I've joined many that encourage people to sew and make, sharing their designs and creations, showing off to their heart's content, and it's really wonderful to see how enthusiastic others are, apart from me. There are groups that advise and suggest ways to upcycle and recycle, making something else out of a stash of fabrics and materials you've got just sitting around gathering dust. Something I do all the time and have done since this sewing journey began, is search for fabric shops on Google (and now yarn) and find out where these places are. Mark and I will book a holiday or a trip somewhere, and I'll spend hours doing my research, finding somewhere to visit in the area. Some of the people in the groups I frequent often reply to my posts asking for recommendations, giving me their own take on a particular shop, and this always creates a conversation within the community about places that are definitely worth a visit, or alternatively, places definitely worth avoiding! Something I started doing recently is make videos of the shops I visit and take lots of photos to share on these groups, along with my YouTube channel, and this is a great way to generate more interest and help the shop owners at the same time.

I described myself as a "magpie" earlier on and that's really what I was like. I'd trawl charity shops, markets and fabric stores and buy anything and everything I could get my hands on. If I thought I could make something with something that caught my eye, it would be in my shopping bag before you could say *buy me now*! I was fascinated by how things looked and often didn't consider whether the fabric and materials would even be used. If I liked what I saw, I'd fit it around something and recreate a design, sometimes throw something together of my own creation that had no relevance to a pattern. Suffice to say, in those early days, I'd arrive home completely laden with bags of fabric and find somewhere in the studio to store it, my thoughts on which pattern being somewhat of an afterthought!

As I mentioned in Chapter Four, I heard about a shop in Lincoln called Fabric Corner. It was tucked away in a corner, naturally, in Cornhill Market. Mark and I headed into Lincoln and went to the market where we came across a stall, quite small in size, but that contained some stunning fabric and I found a roll in pale blue with a line of elephants designed on it. I a bought a metre and even bought a plan to go with it, with the intention of making my godson Henry, a shirt. It was mandarin collared and I have to admit I was very proud of my achievement. I held it aloft and imagined Henry wearing it, hopefully looking as proud as I felt, but when I gave it to him to try on, it was far too small for him—about three sizes too small, to be precise! And so, I bagged it up with other items I'd made that hadn't turned out how they were supposed to, and dropped it off at one of the charity shops in town.

But going back to that little stall on Cornhill Market, the lady who'd served me told me about the actual shop made with bricks and mortar, and gave us directions to its whereabouts, and as soon as I'd put my market stall purchase away, Mark and I set off down the road to find what would become my favourite shop. Kay, the owner, ran the shop, and my eyes lit up when I walked through the door. A little bell jingled and I must have looked like a kid in a sweetshop when she popped up from behind the counter and greeted us with a huge grin. I could see from the second we locked eyes that we'd see more of each other as she gave both Mark and I a warm welcome into her beautiful treasure trove of the finest materials I'd ever seen. Filled with fabrics of all designs and patterns, so many colours in different shades, shelves and counters displaying sewing items that made my head explode into silent squeals of delight.

After that initial meeting, Kay and I became firm friends and we'd share stories about our personal lives. When her son was very ill, her family came together and helped out, and when she told me that, it was just one of the many reasons why I felt we had so much in common.

Next door to Fabric Corner is a wonderfully enchanting coffee shop called Craftea Café, where customers gather regularly not just for a hot drink and a piece of cake, but to share their creations, too. It would look odd if a customer in that café didn't have a craft project in their hands, whiling away the hours chatting and creating and drinking coffee in between. I even ran a workshop there once, a lovely way to get to know people, and now, whenever I visit Fabric Corner or that little crafty café, I end up spending ages chatting to people and sharing advice and my latest designs.

Kay's shop came in very handy during spring of 2018 when I received a response to an application I'd made to appear on a television show. The producer was interested in chatting to me more and I waited a few more weeks for them to contact me again and discuss what I'd be required to do. It involved me presenting some garments that I'd previously made so they could assess my suitability and I spent quite some time contemplating over what those garments would be. My thoughts were whether I should show them items that would make me stand out, perhaps appear out of the ordinary and not something any of the other candidates would take to their interview, or would it be better to stick to the "norm" and show something a little less flamboyant and perhaps more ordinary. In the end, I chose items that I could make that wouldn't make me look like I was pretending to be someone I wasn't. I wanted to come across with confidence and just show them who I really was.

I bought the fabric and materials from Fabric Corner, and made a skirt called Arielle, by Tilly and the Buttons. It was a brand I knew very well. The colour was a bottle-green and was knee-length, and I loved how it looked. For clarity, my description of the skirt is an asymmetric pencil or mini-skirt with an adorable button opening to one side, long darts and a high waistline to create a figure-hugging shape. I lined it in a grey, non-static fabric and down the side I attached eight oversized red buttons and a little gold embroidery detail on each. I used an embroidery design for the hem lining, which consisted of a sequence of tulip flowers stitched along it.

I also made a man's shirt from fabric that was so cheap at just a few pounds per metre. By the time I'd finished it, however, adding endless patterned pieces together and attaching a remnant of fabric from a dress that I had in one of my stash drawers, it looked very expensive and I was thrilled with it. I realised, while making that shirt, that I'd held my breath quite a lot throughout the buttonhole creation in the hope that, like so many sewists assume, will be the magic to making the perfect item. That shirt is still in my dad's wardrobe and it comes out on special occasions like holidays or parties. It had been a challenge to make, but was so worth it, especially when Dad modelled it for me, tucked into a pair of denim jeans and wearing brown shoes. It makes him look incredibly sophisticated!

It was around May when I went down to London to meet with the producer, armed with my precious garments and a huge smile. The chance to meet with industry experts was just what I needed, and it was the chance I had hoped would come my way for some time. I couldn't wait to talk to like-minded sewists, people who knew my craft and were as passionate about what they did as I was. It's always so important to be told you're good at something—the encouragement those words give when you might be doubting yourself a little can change a person's outlook considerably. Because of things that were going on at home, I suppose my insecurities back then were clouding my judgement on my sewing ability, and to chat to people at that meeting and watch them smile and nod and meticulously examine my items meant so much to me. I knew those conversations would be the start of something special and even though I didn't get through to the final stage where I would be invited to appear on television, the words that Jennifer Taylor had said to me at her *Make and Take* workshop at Doncaster Racecourse back in 2015 were prevalent in my mind:

Lucy Picksley

*'If you want something, don't wait around for a
TV show; instead, just make it happen.'*

Another creation I was immensely proud of at that time was my "Healing Bag". Scouring charity shops once again, I came across a pair of denim jeans and a man's brown leather jacket, which fascinated me probably more than anything I'd bought to date. I kept imagining whoever had donated that coat to be wearing it, slipping his hands in the pockets on a cold winter's day, trying desperately to keep them warm. Something really touched me about that coat and as I examined it and the ideas of what I would make with it started to flow, I knew that without a doubt I could never have removed those pockets from the front. Whatever I made with the material itself, the pockets would remain and I would weave them into the design to give the item a more personal touch. I got the charity items back to the studio and laid them on the table, planning and cutting and all the time thinking about that man and his warm hands.

And so the bag began to come to life; a new item being upcycled from an old leather jacket that was no longer wanted. I used some curtain material to line the inside and the denim was attached to the leather on the outside, the pocket proudly on show, by using the Sashiko method of stitching, which is a beautiful Japanese craft. I'll never part with that bag; its name tells you it was made as a therapeutic way to escape the troubles that were taking up so much of my head space at that time. But it was also made with love and a sense of mystery, for I'd never know who that jacket belonged to or whose hands were kept warm in those pockets, and that allows my imagination to run away with me whenever I look at it on display in my studio.

Chapter Nine

I love my husband dearly. He is my one. Always has been, through the good times as well as the tough. Over the past eighteen years, our main priority and concern has been the health and happiness of our boys and they have taken up a lot of our time and attention as most parents will know. Mark is the man who supports me and loves me, holds me when I am crying, helps me to bed when I've had a few too many, and the man who makes me a hot water bottle when I feel unwell. He's the man who, for twenty-two years has been right by my side cheering me on or protecting me from life's monsters ...
"Milatos"

In May 2018, I found myself in hospital with an illness that was eventually put down to stress. I realised we had a long road ahead and whilst all the personal issues were affecting us as a family, I had physical issues going on that were exacerbated by the constant stress I was under. Sewing was still my escapism and I was now enjoying my new studio and the occasional workshop, plus meeting new people who seemed just as keen to improve their creativity as I was. But even the house was suffering in so far as we had a major leak in the main bathroom and even though it had been newly fitted, it all had to be ripped out because the shower tray had cracked and caused extensive damage. We'd also had a new kitchen and the upheaval from that hadn't been ideal, either. My mind was in chaos, just like the house, and it was glaringly obvious when I look back that the shower tray wasn't the only thing broken. I was, too. I tried to persevere, keep going, taking Brady to his riding lessons, which he thoroughly enjoyed.

My doctor was worried about me and not just because of physical stuff going on, but because of the mental angst that was prevalent yet beneath the surface. He wanted to know about my family and the boys and he dug deep, asking about my personal feelings and how I truly felt about Brady's diagnosis. I cried whilst telling him the truth, that I felt monumental guilt that my beautiful boy is "different" and couldn't enjoy a normal birthday with his friends because only two of them bothered to turn up. I told the doctor that I would lay down my life for both of my sons, and that Brady's response to me when I said that was, 'I hope you don't die.' He didn't understand the true depth of meaning behind that statement, even though he would be lost without me. 'All I want is for him to love me back and show me love,' I told the doctor. 'I'm so selfish, I know.'

Perhaps the doctor had been the right person to talk to, maybe he'd heard it before from people with similar illnesses as my own, most of which were brought on by stress. And amazingly, not long after that conversation with the kind-hearted professional, I began to feel a little better, not mentally, but physically. My guilt was ridiculous, I know that now, and I resented the thoughts I had to endure that my boy was "disabled". In my eyes, he's perfect, just like his younger brother. Mark has so many worries too, about the same things I do, yet he supported me and held me up like he always does.

Whilst still in hospital, I wrote a letter to that doctor to thank him for being so kind to me, for listening to me and understanding that there were things happening in my life way deeper than I'd dared to venture, adding that he had helped me accept that I could get through all this. That we, as a family could get through it and move forward. As we left the hospital after I had been discharged, the doctor shook my hand and it felt so sincere. It was a moment of acknowledgement between us, an expression of mutual understanding as his eyes told me that I would never be alone.

My journal entry for 21st May 2018 would seem more like a to-do list, until I wound the clock back and explained why I'd written this list:

> *Police*
> *De Aston*
> *Castlewood Academy*
> *Community Paediatrics*
> *Doctor's*

Two days after I was discharged from the hospital on Sunday, 6th May, the phone rang just as we'd tucked ourselves in bed and were getting prepared for hopefully a good night's sleep.

'Why's Brady on my doorstep?' It was Mark's mum.

The fact was, Brady had been really difficult all day, as usual pushing boundaries and winding us all up to the point where we were exasperated with his behaviour. It turned out that he'd planned to leave the house that night, turn up at his nan's, and announce how much he hated us. By Monday morning, I simply couldn't take any more. I went to see my GP, who signed me off work for a month with stress, and all I felt at that time was embarrassment. I knew deep down how bad things had got, but to have to accept it by being given a sick note wasn't something I was proud of. Things had hit rock bottom and my mental health was in the worst state it's ever been in.

The atmosphere in the house was simply unbearable and we were constantly walking on eggshells, frightened of speaking to each other and scared to death of talking to Brady in case we said the wrong thing and he had another meltdown. I remember being so anxious when I went to bed, almost sleeping with one eye open and being terrified that Brady would leave the house again. One night I heard a noise and jumped out of bed, almost throwing myself into his room and onto his bed, where I held him and told him how frightened I was of him running away. It was the wrong thing to have done, of course, and it only made things worse. His behaviour was now escalating to something beyond our control, and as a darkness descended on him one day when unable to manage his temper, we found him with his hands wrapped around Haydn's neck. We separated them but shortly after, Mark and I were outside and he locked the doors before laying into Haydn again, shouting obscenities, throwing things around the room in a rage before hitting a huge ball into Haydn's face with no remorse. It was excruciating to witness and when, on the following Monday morning, he yet again hurt his brother, the pain I felt couldn't be explained.

'He's really scaring me, Mummy,' Haydn said, and that made me realise that enough was enough, we couldn't continue being scared of our own son or our youngest being scared of his older brother.

As Mark and I felt it might help for someone in authority to speak to Brady about the danger that now seemed to be surrounding our family, I rang the police again that morning and was told an officer would visit with Brady at half-past-three, after school. When I went to collect him, I'd felt obliged to let the school know what had happened, and to be honest, I was dreading what the outcome of that would be. His teacher had asked Brady if he felt bad about what he'd done to Haydn, and the answer had been a resounding *No*. Mr Higgins, the teacher, saw what we saw—no remorse. Though fortunately, that isn't the case now as you read this book.

We opened the door to PC Green later that afternoon, who came in and spoke to Brady in a calm yet authoritative manner, explaining how wrong it was what he'd done, giving him a stiff warning that if the physical and verbal abuse didn't stop, the next visit a police officer would be making would be to put him in handcuffs and show him the insides of a police station cell. Brady was silent when the officer left, but something that really touched me was when PC Green offered to take him fishing, obviously something that would perhaps calm our son and give him something else to concentrate on. We all just wanted to help him, be there for him, show him how much we cared.

It was inevitable by now that Brady needed to start his medication and once again, I chased up the appointments to try and get things moving. Horse riding was helping him and we started taking him to the stables for half a day each week where he got friendly with Jack, a boy who had also been diagnosed with autism and spent a lot of time with the horses as his therapy. As the months progressed, the riding sessions increased to six hours—three hours over two afternoons—Andrew, the instructor, told us he was very proud of Brady and of how much he'd learned. There's no doubt that he's a completely different child when he's around the horses. My dad bought him his first riding hat, which he wore with utter pride and truly looked the part as he sat on Peter, his horse, and cantered him around the arena.

It was nearing the end of May when I felt some respite as Brady had one of his better days and we took my friend Fiona's dogs for a walk. We strolled along the riverbank, chatting away and then stopped for a while and had a cold drink. This was the "real" Brady, the young man who we knew was always there beneath the temper and the meltdowns and the shouting and screaming. Like Haydn had said some time back, it was his condition that made him do and say the things he did, not Brady himself. We all knew that. These quality times we spent together were so incredibly precious for many reasons, not least because we would always remind ourselves of how grown up our youngest son was by acknowledging his brother's difficulties.

Because of the worry we now had where Brady and Haydn being together was concerned, the doctors and police advised us not to leave them on their own without our supervision, and ideally not at all. It was a very tough time as both boys needed childcare due to both

Mark and I working, and this meant we had to separate them and arrange for two lots of childminders. Our parents didn't want or need that level of responsibility; Mark and I were accountable for our sons and it came to be that each weekend, we would split the family up where I had one and Mark the other. This meant, of course, that we saw very little of each other for two days a week and we'd go our own way, doing different age-appropriate activities with each one and really hoping it wouldn't need to go on for too long.

It was draining us both and it actually felt very alien to what we were used to. Our marriage was and always has been very strong and we do as much as we can together. But we had to protect Haydn and it was important to support Brady as much as possible. He was suffering terribly with everything going on in his young mind, trying so hard to make sense of who he was becoming. It isn't just the parents of special needs children that suffer and find everyday life an uphill struggle, but the child or children are desperately reaching out for help—not really knowing why.

However, this arrangement worked and even though it completely ground our social life to a halt, Mark and I could at least see that we'd made the right decision. It obviously was far from ideal as we hardly saw each other, and we were very rarely together at all, except at night once the boys had gone to bed. We were worn out, and that's no lie.

Something I did enjoy was meeting Brady from the school bus once a week and taking him to Costa. It was just the two of us, spending much-needed quality time together. He always chose a caramel latte and either chocolate fudge cake or a brownie. On some of our outings, Brady would sit at the table and not say one word, for the whole hour we were there. Occasionally, he would say the odd thing to me that would often leave me startled. It could be just about something that happened at school, or what he'd had for lunch, but it would completely brighten up my day. Once or twice, probably no more, he would open up and talk about his feelings, but I never led the conversation; I always let Brady do that. I'd just sit there, drinking my coffee and soaking up the moments we had together, smiling inside as me and my boy looked like the most normal mother and son in the world.

Whilst this book was being written, Brady mentioned those precious times to me and told me he misses our trips to Costa, and to hear him say that is one of the most special things he's ever said to me.

Chapter Ten

Newbold Comyn was the place for adventure and where there's adventure, there's a rucksack with snacks to keep us going through the day. It was straight down the hill that me and the twins wanted to go because there, was a hidden treasure that had stood for the longest time. The "Old Steamy", a dilapidated steam engine that kids used to play on, was hidden away in the undergrowth, long since abandoned by its owners. The poor old girl was a bit tatty and covered in graffiti, but this was our chance to don our pretend stationmaster's whistle, straighten our caps, and take our passengers for a ride across the countryside ...
"Newbold Rucksack"

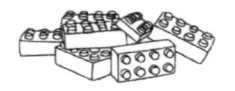

School started again in September and Brady went into Year 8 at the age of twelve. It was good to see he was making the effort to get back into a routine—something autism totally needs is routine, and we always tried hard, and still do, to maintain this in the hope of keeping as much calm as possible in the home. On the downside, he managed to land himself three detentions in just six days but he also received a certificate for lots of positives, too, and we decided to focus on that. He was working hard in English and doing really well in Maths, Art classes were going great, and he was showing a lot of enthusiasm in Science. He did talk a lot about a bully at school, though, and when this boy started to tease Brady, he got a swift kick in the groin, which, even though I would never condone violence, I do feel that sometimes bullies need to be reminded the world doesn't evolve around them.

I had a feeling something more was going on when, for the second time in five days he asked if he could stay at home. Whether the bullying was affecting him we don't know, but he did say he was being teased again. He was getting on with his homework and didn't seem much trouble at home for a while, so we felt we could maybe relax a little. The school did email me a few times telling me about issues that were happening around Brady, but we managed to talk to him and sort things out because by the beginning of October, he came home one afternoon and asked if he could go on a school trip to Germany. Mark and I felt it would do him good, a change of scenery and something to look forward to, and so we agreed that he could go. However, the school were somewhat negative with their approach when we gave the go-ahead saying it all depended on how many pupils wanted to go and also their behaviour.

Brady must have really wanted to go on that trip because those conditions saw him working hard over the coming days on his homework, particularly his art, which was very impressive. I'd been thinking about Christmas presents and had come up with the idea of buying him his own laptop rather than having to use mine all the time; I was sure he could be trusted to look after it.

One evening he got back from school and announced he was meeting his friends outside the shop, and they would be hanging out together on their bikes. As always,

I insisted he took his mobile phone for emergencies and told him to be home in one hour and not to go in the woods. The nights were closing in and I really didn't want him hanging around the streets after dark. We'd been through it too often—the worry and the angst about where he was, what he was doing, was he lying in a ditch somewhere; one of our jobs as parents is to worry, and that was certainly something we excelled at!

Twenty minutes after he should have got home, it had gone dark and naturally I started to wonder where he was. I went out and had a walk to the shop where he told me he'd be, where, of course, he wasn't, and so I made my way to the woods instead. I guess me saying he couldn't go there prompted him to go, kids often do things we tell them not to just to find out *why* we're telling them not to, and as I thought, there he was, in the woods on his own. His bike had a puncture and he'd dumped it, but the worse part of it was that his friends had abandoned him, maybe gone home, I don't know, but I wasn't happy that he'd once again gone against my word and ended up in the very place I'd asked him not to go.

I got him home and he was clearly in a mood by now. But, nonetheless, I gave him my laptop and let him go online to do a test he needed to do for a class at school. Because of the puncture, I guess, and me having words with him about how worried I'd been and the fact I shouldn't have to venture out in the dark searching for him, his concentration was perhaps at a low point and he got some of the questions wrong—some which I presume he would normally have known the answer to. That resulted in another meltdown where he punched the screen of my laptop, causing damage to it. I used that laptop for working from home, and I really couldn't risk it being broken. I'd trusted him to respect it, and even though he often did, it raised the question of whether he would actually be responsible should I buy him his own for Christmas.

We had an appointment with a community paediatric at the beginning of October, and Brady was willing to accept medication. We'd spoken to him about it and considered the long-term impact, the side effects and the consequences. He was on his best behaviour while we were there and engaged well with the paediatrician. He was asked a lot of questions and I was actually quite proud of him as he answered politely. His T-Score was measured, which in layman's terms is a system used to measure a child's percentile on the autism spectrum. Scores over 76 rank in the "severe" autism range, while scores of between 60 and 75 indicate mild to moderate autism. I knew I'd done the right thing in having him referred. His results came back:

Inattention:	90
Impulsivity:	*Off the chart*
Defiance and aggression:	89
Peer relations:	89
Executive functioning:	71
Learning:	42

This showed the professionals that Brady needed the help we had requested and it was happening just at the right time. He was prescribed Methylphenidate, which is a medication for children with ADHD and impulsive behaviour, and once settled into the system, allows them to concentrate better. Brady didn't have a problem with it and said, 'I'm fine with it,' which was a huge relief to us, as there was no way we would have forced him to take it should he have been unwilling. Of course, I was worrying about the side effects and if it would work for him, but we knew it was the right thing to do. If it slowed down his reactions a little then it could only be a good thing, enabling him to perhaps think for a few more moments before lashing out with a knee-jerk reaction whenever something didn't go his way. I wrote in my journal that day, *This doesn't make me a bad mother, does it?* The guilt we feel as parents is phenomenal when really, all we're trying to do is our very best to keep our children safe, give them a good start in life, and offer them all the support they could ever need. But yet still we feel guilty if something out of the norm needs to happen, something that could potentially destroy our idea of being the perfect parent and having the perfect kids—neither of which exist and never will.

When he did eventually start taking the medication, a few weeks later, he hated it. The effects were immediate and we quickly noticed a difference in him. It seemed to have quietened him down and we could see he just wasn't himself. He even told us as much when we talked it through sometime later. School did report, however, that his ability to stay focused and on task had improved, though he was showing a reluctance to do his homework. I remember one weekend a few months after he'd started on the meds, I took him out in the car and he told me that he wanted to feel like himself again, even if that did mean going off the rails occasionally.

Hummingbirds and Kaleidoscopes

We noticed a decrease in his weight because he wasn't eating as much, his appetite having taken a spiral, and so we had a discussion about it with Mark and decided it would be okay for him to stay off the medication at weekends. Our reason behind this thinking was that if it helped him perform better at school throughout the week and also at home doing his homework, then we might all find it easier to cope better with any issues at weekends. I can definitely say it worked well.

Just days after this appointment, on the following Saturday, he once more went off adventuring on his bike—puncture now mended—and unfortunately came off it. Poor Brady was injured, his hands bleeding, and he was also covered in mud after falling off. It worried him so much that he knocked on the front door of the nearest property and asked for help, but the homeowner dismissed him and told him to go away. I can understand why some people wouldn't take kindly to a twelve-year-old appearing at their door looking somewhat dishevelled and filthy, but honestly, that did upset me that they couldn't at least offer to phone his parents. Unfortunately, by Sunday, Brady's mood had descended into a huge meltdown and because of the amount of times he'd been told recently about coming home late and disobeying our instructions—for his own safety—he lost it. He was out of control, shouting and swearing at us and eventually climbed out of his bedroom window and scaled down the outside wall.

We caught up with him and brought him back inside, handed him a glass of water and one of his magic pills, the Phenergan we'd been able to obtain from the chemist some time ago, bearing in mind it wouldn't affect the

Methylphenidate. It calmed him down and I even told him that if he still hated us, like he kept saying, and wanted to run away again, his dad and I would make provisions. But just twenty minutes later, amazingly, and much to our utter relief, he was sat at the table with Haydn, who was colouring in, building a construction out of Lego. I smiled. It was just a moment of perfection, but one that meant so much to me.

Chapter Eleven

In my opinion, the most beautiful of the Greek Islands must be Zakynthos, or Zante as it's also know, and the town of Tsilivi which holds special memories for me. The first time I travelled there was on Tuesday the 3rd August 2004 for a week of loved-up bliss with my new husband, Mark. It was our honeymoon, our getaway, and it was the best holiday of my entire life. We travelled a few days after our wedding, giving us time to soak up the excitement of the day and do those final bits of packing. We stayed at the Hotel Mediterranee, which wasn't far from the seafront and close to the bars ...
"Tsilivi"

I get asked so often by friends, neighbours, and often family members if I'd mind sewing a button on or mending a zip, take a pair of trousers up or do general alterations to a garment that someone's bought. It might not fit them anymore, or they might have bought it in a sale at a knock down price, knowing it would need altering but perhaps deciding to get it done rather than pay full price for their regular size. It happens! I know I'm not alone when I say this as I've had this conversation with many sewists who get asked the same. 'It won't take you long,' they say, having no idea how long it will take, and how fiddly it might be, and how much pressure it will become if I don't do it exactly how they want it done. So, no. More often than not, I don't do alterations.

However, occasionally, I've been challenged with something that I just can't pass up on, a unique chance to make a difference, to help someone that you know will not only be a good deed, but that will leave you feeling in a good place as a little spark ignites from within. This is exactly what happened with my neighbour, Sophie, in February 2019. I'd taken in a parcel for her from Royal Mail and she knocked on my door when she got home to collect it. When I handed it over to her, she told me it was her wedding dress. I was quite surprised in all honesty, because the parcel was quite small and I couldn't imagine a wedding dress being wrapped up into such a small bundle. But she was very excited and thanked me for taking it in, then shot back to her house smiling like a Cheshire cat. A few minutes later, Sophie messaged me and asked if I'd go to her house and have a look at the dress. Before she showed me, she explained that she was on a tight budget and it was all she could afford, and I was quite glad she'd said that. Because when I looked at it I simply couldn't believe anyone could sell a dress so awful to a blushing bride-to-be, expecting them to gush over it and get excited about wearing it on their big day.

It was truly awful, made from cheap fabric and just looked to me as though the material could be highly flammable. Sophie was naturally disappointed and we went on to have a chat about what type of dress she could buy instead. As we all know, weddings are ridiculously expensive and she'd given herself a small budget to use to find the perfect dress. But this most definitely wasn't it. She'd bought it online after seeing a photograph that she said was so much nicer than the garment she'd by now discarded on a chair. Looks can often be deceiving when we view items of clothing online because it's difficult to determine the quality of the fabric, whether buttons line up to holes, if zips work properly, and so many other areas that get overlooked if you're just trying to envision yourself wearing it. I agreed to help Sophie that day and do my own research, looking for suitable dresses that I could see her perhaps wearing and that I knew would be made from high quality fabric and not the cheap and nasty stuff that she'd been sent. I went back home and spent the rest of the afternoon and into the evening looking through dresses, as did she, and we pinged messages back and forth to show each other what we'd found. Eventually, we came across one that looked like it could be "the one", and Sophie tapped on the *Buy* button and parted with £40. Extremely cheap for a wedding dress, I admit, but I agreed it looked okay and could be altered if necessary.

The dress was delivered to Sophie a few days' later, accompanied by a handwritten note to say they'd also included a lace bolero in the package, that contained sequins stitched onto it. It was a beautiful dress and definitely a bargain for what she'd paid, with a zip at the back, a strapless design, the bodice fitted with rouching to the front, and the skirt that gently swept to the floor. It was an exciting moment as you can imagine, and she went to try it on, but as she stepped into it and started to pull it up her frame, it became obvious it was too small. Far too small, in fact. Sophie was mortified and burst into tears. Money was starting to run out for the wedding budget and this was just another blow that she didn't need. When I asked if she'd put her trust in me and allow me to have a go at making some alterations, she nodded and attempted to smile. I promised her we'd sort it out somehow and as she had very few options left, and she agreed I could take it away and work my magic.

Before I left, I asked her to try it on again for me so I could see where it needed altering. I needed to figure out exactly what would be required, how I could make changes to it by not taking away the design too much. The main problem was the back where the zip was. It needed an extra five inches across the top to allow a breath to be taken and it was this that became my biggest challenge.

I very carefully unpicked the long zip that ran down the centre back and disposed of it. Taking the lace bolero, I cut a sleeve off and lay it flat. Looking at the piece of fabric, I saw that the edge was scalloped and finished off quite beautifully, and with some rotation and careful placement it could sit as a dignity panel across the back. To ensure the whole thing stayed in place, it still needed a way to fasten. To achieve this, I made endless rouleau loops that were stitched down each edge where the zip had once been and then sewed the dignity panel in. Metres of narrow ribbon were threaded through the loops, starting at the top and working their way down to the bottom where they were tied and settled. As a finishing touch, I sewed Swarovski crystals down each side of the back openings and this gave it a pretty and purposeful finish.

I was as thrilled as Sophie was when she tried it on and it fit her perfectly. She looked stunning and it made her even more excited about her forthcoming wedding. Unfortunately, the big day had been booked to take place on 18th April 2020, when we went into the first Covid lockdown, and so she and her husband-to-be had to postpone it. It was utter bad luck that they had to do that a few times due to the pandemic, but eventually, on 30th April 2022, their special day finally arrived and she wore that dress, that had cost so little in wedding-dress terms, with the utmost pride. My gift to Sophie had been to make her day perfect as she dazzled the congregation and blew her husband away.

I guess I'm not one to do things by halves, but this was and is exactly the type of alteration I simply love to do. When I'm not asked but simply trusted to be creative, this gives me encouragement to tackle anything. You can't put a monetary value on seeing someone smile because you've been a big part of making them happy. Especially on their wedding day.

Another proud make for me was when I helped my friend's son, Ben. He had a serious accident in August 2019 where his motorbike collided with a lorry and he was airlifted to hospital. He was in a pretty bad way and it took several operations to save his right leg, which had been severely damaged in the accident. He'd suffered an open fracture of the tibia and fibula, smashed the patella, and damaged the bottom of the femur. The outcome looked dire and even though he got through the surgery with his leg still intact, he had to wear a huge frame wrapped around his lower leg that the surgeon informed him could be something he'd need for the next three years. Ben was obviously devastated as it was going to mean many alterations to the way he'd lived his life, apart from which, he wasn't too enamoured at the thought of having a leg frame on view that would make him feel self-conscious and probably attract a lot of unwanted staring. He had high hopes to be up and about as quickly as possible; something I admire about him.

When his mum approached me with an idea of perhaps making something to cover the frame, as well as keeping his leg warm, I knew it was something I wanted to help with. The colder months were almost upon us, and so I had a good think about how to go about this next project to hopefully put a smile on someone's face again.

The idea was a pair of bespoke trousers. Ben's small frame had to be considered as well as adding extra space for the frame that was approximately nine inches diameter. I won't deny it was a challenge at first because I really wanted to help him, and it did cause a few sleepless nights where I'd lie awake with all sorts of patterns, designs, fabrics and ideas racing through my head, determined to get it right. Eventually, I had that lightbulb moment and came up with something that I was sure would do the trick.

I made Ben's first pair of trousers as a trial run, simply hoping they would fit and I could perhaps refine my skills to go on and make a much better pair. I was of the impression they were okay—just okay—but Ben, to my great relief, was absolutely over the moon with them, and this spurred me on to make another pair that I'd been thinking about, only this time out of a denim fabric. I intended to make a perfect pair of jeans for him, ones he could parade out in and not feel at all self-conscious.

Hummingbirds and Kaleidoscopes

One thing I had to take into account was the fact that Ben had lots of hospital and physio appointments to attend over those first few months, and it was paramount that he had easy access to whatever trousers I created for him rather than having to struggle taking them off, then struggle again putting them back on. He needed to retain his dignity whilst he was recovering, and the last thing he would have wanted was to need constant help from medical staff as he wrestled with his clothes. I obtained the pattern called *Eve* that I wanted to work from, which would fit in well with the size of his left leg, and used Merchant and Mills fabric. For the right leg, the one he'd damaged, I inserted a nine-inch strip of fabric that ran the full length, and then sandwiched between the seams I inserted an open-ended zip, one similar to a jacket, so it could be done up above the frame and the fabric be pulled in to give the trouser leg some shape. I pleated the excess fabric at the top of the leg at the side and attached a button to the outside. To the lower leg, the excess fabric simply draped over the frame, which was intended as a disguise and hopefully prevent the unnecessary stares that he was quite anxious about. I also added plenty detail to the garment that you'd expect to see on a quality pair of jeans, such as back pockets with fancy stitching, top stitching throughout, and a side fastening waistband.

He loved them, and I was absolutely delighted. I particularly admired him for the work he put in to his rehabilitation and it turned out that the predicted three years the surgeons had suggested he would need to wear the frame for, ended up being less than eight months. It was a miracle, but he was determined to get back to normal. Ben is a great inspiration to other people who find themselves in such an unfortunate position. I did shed a few tears when he wrote the following beautiful testimonial:

> *Before the jeans, I could only really wear shorts, and even getting those on could be difficult. When I was wearing shorts constantly, I was pretty paranoid about going out and increasing the risk of infection. There were also a lot of questions and comments made, and it felt like people were constantly staring at my leg. I hate standing out, so having the option to hide the most unusual, visible part of my injury was a life saver.*
>
> *Shorts also made the prospect of going back to work even more difficult.*
>
> *I was in love with the trousers! They made me warm, clean, and much less self-conscious. From a distance they looked exactly like normal trousers, and the main giveaway of my injury was the crutches! I could go outside on walks, and if there was only a brief glance at me it didn't look like anything had happened. I really liked being able to wear smarter-looking clothes again, rather than jogger shorts only. Jeans are my go-to clothing option, so having them helped me mentally recover and feel I was getting back to myself.*
>
> *Lucy also made some smarter work trousers, which were excellent for me to go into the office and see people without feeling that I massively*

stood out. They also demonstrated my wounds could be covered, which meant it was more hygienic for me to return. Not being at work was having a huge impact on my mental health. For me, what was special about the adaptation was the time spent ensuring the jeans were perfect for me. Lucy knows that all people are different, and providing a bespoke service really tailored to my needs.

Chapter Twelve

There she was, on the shelf waiting for me to buy her as a gift for my mum. It was a pottery cat that I knew she would love and adore just like I did. I took her to the till and had her wrapped up in tissue paper, which was exchanged for a handful of coppers. I took her home to Mum and gave her this thing of beauty, excited to know it would make it onto the mantelpiece—her pride and joy. How was I to know that she hated cats just as much as those flowers, or weeds as they were, that I brought home for her on my walks back from the park when we lived on Exham Close? I might not always get it right, but my heart's in the right place ...

"Crownway Shopper"

It was September 2019 when I received a message from Haydn's old childminder, Vanessa. She'd been a wonderful carer to him and had taught him so much; life skills and manners, how to behave in public and how to make friends with his peers. She wanted my advice, asking for the best place to buy a sewing machine for her teenage daughter, Abbie, who had recently started showing an interest in sewing. She also asked if I could offer lessons too, and that was something I was more than happy to say yes to.

We made arrangements for Abbie to come over that following Thursday evening for a two-hour lesson starting at 6pm. She was shy and I did suggest to

Vanessa, her mum, that it would be absolutely fine if she wanted to sit in on the lessons and perhaps be a familiar face for Abbie. But much to mine and Vanessa's surprise, Abbie jumped straight out of the car at my house and was eager to get started, without her mum in tow! That first lesson was awesome as she chose to make the Cleo dungaree dress by Tilly and the Buttons. The fabric was navy blue and I remember it being Vanessa's first photo to display on her Facebook page, receiving an abundance of comments and praise from friends and family.

This shy girl was starting to come out of her shell, and each week I was noticing a change in her — subtle in some respects, but there all the same. A few weeks into her lessons, her mum and dad bought her a sewing machine, her first, the Singer Start. That told me how keen she was to pursue this and I wanting nothing more than to help her achieve the ambition she so clearly now had. She was hooked, and it was a pleasure to watch her eyes light up and see how eager she was every Thursday at 6pm when she arrived at the studio. Her parents sent me lots of lovely messages expressing how amazing it was to see Abbie so enthusiastic, telling me she looked forward each week to her lesson with me, and in one of the messages, they asked if I could make a list of what she would need to set up her own workstation in her bedroom. It was a couple of months till Christmas, so I assumed the items I suggested would be on her present list.

It didn't take her long to become independent and not have to rely on me so much. Her growth each week astounded me; I was so proud to watch her flourish in my studio, working on designs we spent time chatting about during our time together. She was now able to self-correct without being directed, how to thread her machine on her own and solve any problems that often crop up. I also noticed the shyness was becoming a thing of the past as she'd open up to me more with every lesson, and even though she wasn't a chatterbox, I felt comfortable with her and felt able to talk to her, listen to her, and just be her friend. We'd talk about our next plan as each project came to an end, and we'd made a shopping list of materials we'd need to make it happen. Abbie enjoyed online shopping with her mum, choosing fabrics against patterns, something I should have done more of in my early days as a sewist! She would always check with me to make sure she was choosing the right fabric before buying it and as we had similar tastes anyway, most of what she chose was what I perhaps would have gone for, too. Her confidence was going from strength to strength, as we'd make the same garment at the large table in the studio, sat side-by-side. One of the items we made together was a Bobbi dress, which is a pinafore dress with buttons straight down the front and lots of pockets on the front panels, as well as two on the bum area. Abbie made hers in grey cord and I made mine in mustard, and as there was enough fabric left over, she went on to make herself a skirt version of the Bobbi dress.

By December, Abbie had saved enough money from her paper round to buy fabric to use for a Christmas present for her mum. It was a beautiful wool waterfall coat called *Bianca* by *Sew Me Something*. I knew the pattern well as I'd made three of the coats for myself, and then another three for my mum, my cousin Sarah, and a colleague of mine who was due to start treatment for cancer. I wanted her to have something warm and snuggly, a coat that would wrap around her body and make her feel safe. Abbie's coat had a grey base and mulberry-red check patterning to it. Two large pockets were attached to the front, and Abbie said these would be used by her mum to put tissues in for the kids she looked after when they'd go on their walks in the cold weather. I imagine when Vanessa opened that gift on Christmas Day, it would have been quite something to see the smile on her face, knowing that her daughter had made it herself with the money she'd earned and saved.

Abbie was so quick to learn. By February of the following year, she'd come as usual for her weekly lesson where we'd chat and I'd demonstrate and teach her more skills, and then she'd take whatever she'd started to make back home and continue at home on her sewing machine that was now set up in her bedroom. In the half-term holiday that month, she made a pinafore dress from start to finish, in a stretch fabric with cross-over straps to the back, and Vanessa sent me a photo of it. I realised then that Abbie probably didn't need my help so much now as she was obviously tearing away on her own, her skills now so advanced that she was able to create a garment from scratch without needing to sit next to me and rely on my tutoring. It was marvellous to see; this once-shy teenager now a young woman with the determination to throw herself into any project and see it through.

Of course, by mid-March, the world closed its doors and life was no longer as we knew it—more of that to come—and I was so relieved that Abbie's confidence *had* grown, because I would have worried otherwise that she may not have carried on. But her eagerness to fulfil this ambition wasn't going to stop her sewing, and in April her parents bought her a new and much more sophisticated sewing machine; a Janome. I was thrilled for her because these are my favourite models and I've used them for years now. Something else that will come later!

When things had calmed down with the dreaded lockdowns and we were able to get back to at least some kind of normality in July, Abbie returned to the studio and we continued our lessons. One of the things that were proving popular at the time was, of course, facemasks, and so she bought lots of fabric and we got to work making batches of them that she would at first give out to her family. But eventually, she started to sell them and was able to make some of the money back that she'd spent on materials.

By the summer, Abbie's skills were even more impressive and we decided to move up a gear and attempt to make one of our most ambitious creations since I'd been teaching her. This was the Farrah jumpsuit by *Sew Over It*. It looked like a modern day version of a boiler suit, though had a more feminine touch to it with an elasticated waist to accentuate the female figure, and was turned up at the ankle cuffs. It had lots of pockets on the thighs as well as on the bum and at the front. Abbie chose a navy-blue colour whilst I went for a coral fabric, and I still wear mine occasionally. We both loved those jumpsuits and received so many compliments from people, on social media and in real life. When Vanessa sent me a message once day saying how amazing Abbie looked in it, I must admit it gave me a lot of pride to know I'd helped her, pride that was also felt by Abbie and her mum.

It wasn't long before she had her own labels printed and started to sew them in all her creations: *Made By Abbie*. I knew how that would have felt because of having my own labels designed five years previously of *Sew Pretty*, and then in 2018 of *Sew Pretty Sew Mindful*. When you see your own label in something knowing how much work you've put into making it, the feeling is one of immense fulfilment, a self-esteem boost that can only encourage you more. Abbie was reaping the rewards of her designs and could now say the same thing as I said when people wanted to know where you got your dress from. 'I made it,' she went on to say, with a little blush at first, graciously accepting the compliment each time.

Another lockdown in October meant that we had to call a halt to the sewing lessons again, but this time it wasn't so frustrating as Abbie had recently started the next chapter of her journey: sixth form college. The course she'd chosen was Art and Textiles, along with A-levels, and the fact she did exceptionally well in these subjects meant she went on to be offered a place at Leeds University where she would later realise her own dreams and ambitions.

In just over a year, my amazing student Abbie, had gone from shy and a lack of confidence, to a young woman with determination, her own label, and a place on the course she had worked incredibly hard to achieve. She'd accomplished so much in such a short space of time, and to say I was proud of her would be an understatement.

Abbie's story didn't end there, though, as now, as these words are being written, she is able to live, work, and sew independently and has reached the ambition she set out to achieve five years previously when she first came to me that Thursday evening, bounding from her mum's car, eager to start making a Cloe dungaree dress. Such an admirable young lady.

Chapter Thirteen

Up and down Northumberland Road we would drive, Mum and Dad in the front of the car, me and the twins in the back. Dad would drive really slow to give us a chance to point out our dream homes. Wisteria climbed up the facades, framing beautiful doorways to which I imagined would lead to magnificent interiors. It's good to daydream; positive affirmations in disguise. A few years' later, we got to have our very own enormous house with concrete pigs front and centre at the top of the driveway. Life began in Lincolnshire as a family of six with the arrival of my younger brother ...
"Northumberland Backpack"

My dad restores and renovates old sewing machines, and in particular, Featherweight 221 and Featherweight 222 machines, that quilting enthusiasts will be familiar with. He's often got a garage full of them waiting to be worked on. Some have been shipped from as far as America, Canada, and even Australia. He runs a very popular Facebook group called *Singer Featherweights UK*, where he has a substantial amount of followers who contact him for advice, suggestions, and how they can get their machines repaired. He's known as "Feather Phil" to some of his clients, and "Doctor Phil" to others. His magical touch and deep understanding of these machines and their historical reference is astounding, and something that his customers love about him. Some of the machines need meticulous repairs, which Dad will do, taking great care and using the utmost professionalism on each one. A lot of them have been passed down to family members, which also makes them sentimental. So his job often becomes a project of love for his clients, making it a wonderful achievement for Dad once he's sent it back and been given the praise he deserves. His renovations include hours of polishing, rubbing in tiny circular motions before he starts to buff the surface with a soft cloth. Many of the machines he gets sent arrive in cases with battered corners and rusty hinges, and the final stages of his work involves making these cases beautiful and shiny again. My mum helps with this, too, though Dad tends to do the locks and hinges. Most of his work is known, in Dad's words, as "A Fully Monty", and I can definitely see what he means. His concentration and precision leaves his customers in awe when they see the quality of his restorations, and those in the UK, no matter how near or far, will drive over to his workshop, leave the machine with him, then drive back once it's finished with utter admiration for the magic he performs on their pride and joy.

I can't tell you how much I wanted one of these machines. Seeing them in Dad's workshop all the time made me yearn to own my own one day, but they are expensive and it wasn't something I really needed anyway. I just loved them with a passion, and loved Dad's enthusiasm as he'd set to work on them.

Christmas Day of 2019, we'd sat in Mum and Dad's living room opening our presents, finished our dinner, had the usual family time of games and laughter and important discussions on how many roast potatoes to cook, when Dad approached me and put a key into my hand. 'Come on,' he said, gesturing with his head for me to follow him. He took me to his workshop, opened the door, and stood aside for me to go in first. Then he pointed to a black box and said, 'Merry Christmas, love.'

I couldn't believe it. Dad had managed to buy a battered old Featherweight 221 that had become such a challenge to renovate, that he'd made an offer to buy it instead, knowing it would be nigh-on impossible to do up. But he'd done his best with it and even though there were lots of scratches and imperfections on it, he knew it would be perfect for me. He also knew I would look after it like it deserved to be looked after, and I would love it not just because it was a machine I'd wanted for such a long time, but because it was a complete surprise given to me by my beloved dad. The lid still had stickers on it from the places it had been to, taken there by its owners, though I did remove them. It was one of the best presents I'd ever been given, up there with Brady's paint-splattered plate and Haydn's vintage sign.

I unclipped the brass locks and slowly opened the lid, my face no doubt lit up with emotion. There she sat, inside the box, looking, to me, absolutely perfect. Her glossy black coating shone, masking the scratches that I no longer saw, and I reached in carefully and lifted her out. The gold lettering of the name *Singer* lifted my heart, along with gold scrolling along each edge, reminding me of an Egyptian design. I put my fingers on the top of the handwheel and turned it gently, then moved them round to the on/off button, a simple mechanism with no fuss and no complicated instructions. A gold badge attached to the machine with the words *The Singer, Manfg Co, Serial number EH243005*, meaning she was built between March and April 1952, made me smile again, as I then unfolded the attached table that are now so old-fashioned in our modern world of sewing. Inside the box also was the original feet for the machine, together with the original handbook and original oil bottle. These items had been manufactured with the machine itself, and the fact they were all included made this stunning piece of brilliance all the more special.

I wanted to give my beautiful machine a name, and decided it would be *Betty*, after my paternal grandmother. The reason I chose my gran's name was because something was making me feel her charisma through the machine; both Gran and machine had lived a full life, and would have seen so much throughout it. It hit me hard to lose Gran. My grief was excruciating, and once more I turned to sewing to escape the constant grief that I felt. It was only right that I made something in her memory using *Betty*, and that was to be a patchwork quilt that took me away to a whole new world as I spent hours getting to know my gorgeous machine. I devised the pattern from scratch, just making it up as I went along, and it grew and grew until it became a much bigger project than I had first set out to do.

The first step to making the quilt was to buy the fabrics and materials, and I found myself in a shop I'd never been in before called Wisteria Patchwork in the village of Swinderby in Lincolnshire. There, I spent several hours looking through different fabrics, choosing colours and patterns, and trying to envision what I would do with them, how I would sew them together so they matched and looked like they were meant to be exactly where I'd positioned each square. I placed the fabrics on a long table to make sure I was on the right track with my ideas, until I finally had the perfect combination I was looking to achieve. Most of the fabrics I chose were Liberty, with other blender fabrics mixed in. The colours I'd gone for were blues and white, with accents of gold flashing through.

The whole project was led from how I felt, my emotions at the time, and when I started the process of sewing up log cabin squares, I just let the stitches flow until I felt it was right to stop. I had no patterns or designs, nothing illustrated that I could work from. It was purely my imagination that spurred me on. Once the log cabins were made, I sub-cut them into small pieces which gave me the freedom to rotate each one before piecing them back together. Around the outside of the log cabins, I pinned half-square triangles together in alternating colours that when they were turned around, created different images. The options were endless, as once you make half-square triangles, it makes the project so versatile for any quilt designer, enabling their imagination to run away with them as they see a beautiful piece of craft work come together. I added sashes of navy and gold to the borders, and this completely brought the quilt to life.

Working on *Betty* was an absolute joy. She managed the process extremely well, easily piecing together tiny, neat stitches, and no matter how big and heavy the quilt got, my trusty old sewing machine took it all in her stride. I just love listening to her whirring as the bobbin winds, and hearing the tinkering sounds she emits as the stitches are applied. Being a fast machine, it's important to get to grips with the foot control also, to ensure an even, sensible pace as you work the longer stretches of fabric.

When I finished stitching the patchwork, I sent the quilt off to Annette, a professional and very experienced long-armed quilter, to apply the finishing touches. This is a process where batting is sandwiched between the upper and lower layer, and beautiful flourishes of stitching design is added to keep it all together, making sure it'll stand the test of time. I was quite touched when, after Annette had finished the work, rather than posting it back to me she got in her car and drove from Humber to my house in Lincolnshire to hand deliver it. Once I had it back in my possession, the final stage began where I hand sewed the binding. Eventually finished, I held the quilt against me, reminiscing about Gran, before I put it away for a few months and began my next project.

Chapter Fourteen

Gran, known as Betty to some and Elizabeth to others, was my rock, my hero, and someone I looked up to. She was always so glamorous, styled her hair just so, and was never without makeup. She taught me how to check my hair from the back and how to add a touch of lipstick — on my eyes — if I needed to accentuate my look. She cooked a mean Sunday roast, poured boiling water over her cereal, and did a crossword every single day. Before she passed away, she held on tight to her purse, empty of money but filled with memories; photos of loved ones that she stroked each day, willing those memories to come back. She was a true legend ...
"Elizabeth"

My gran had been suffering with dementia for the previous two years and we'd watched her decline before our eyes. Then, just mere days into the new year, she passed away, and it was as though she'd waited until my dad had given me the Featherweight 221 sewing machine for Christmas and made the decision on naming her *Betty*. None of us had any idea that Gran only had days to live, so it was particularly poignant that I'd decided to call my treasured possession after the woman who had been a huge influence in my life. She had long forgotten who I was whenever I went to visit her, but we knew it couldn't be taken to heart. Though, strangely, the very last time

I *did* visit her, she told me she loved me and right there and then, I simply knew that would be the last time I would ever see her.

I was particularly close to Gran and it destroyed me when she lost her battle with the very cruel condition that turned her from one of the most vibrant and flamboyant characters I'd ever known, to someone who no longer recognised who I was. Her life had been so incredibly eventful and everyone she met had the utmost admiration for her. She'd spent many years being a performer on stage, in shows and plays, and even singing for the troops in the second world war. Her beautiful operatic soprano voice would fill you with emotion as she belted out songs, her confidence shining through, enjoying every moment as she entertained anyone who wanted to watch. She exuded energy in everything she did and I can honestly say she lived her life to the full.

In 1992, when I was just sixteen, I went to live with Gran as I got accepted on a course at Mid Warwickshire College of Further Education studying a BTEC National Diploma in Art and Design. (I specialised in Textile Design and passed with a Merit.) I moved in with her on Sunday 6th September 1992, and even though I don't recall much of what we did together, I do remember the love and warmth she gave to me whilst I lived in her home. We'd often sit in her garden and chat for hours on end, listening to the birdsong and feeling the gentle ambience that was so calming. She had a bird table and I can see her now as I used to look out of my bedroom window, watching her fill up the table with food, always one with nature and the beauty of wildlife. Unlike me, she wasn't a cat lover and would complain if ever one came into the garden. I'm sure it was the thought of them scaring her beloved birds, but she didn't really help herself, especially on a Sunday, when she'd cook a splendid, traditional roast dinner and put the leftovers outside for the birds to feed on!

She loved her Sunday dinners and I would often get up on a Sunday morning as she was preparing it, her radio blaring out with choir music. She always made enough to last into the following Monday, and would wrap clingfilm around each plate to keep it fresh. I can still taste those dinners today, perfection on a plate, accompanied by a sauce of some sort—either bread or onion. She'd also make a delicious pudding that was usually a crumble or a lattice pie, but I was usually too full to manage any!

Something Gran loved to do, apart from sing, was go ballroom dancing and she would often go out on a Friday or Saturday night looking strikingly beautiful in her favourite pleated skirt and glittery top. She'd also wear pointed-toe shoes with heels and would take ages doing her makeup. As she would be getting ready, I'd sit on her bed and watch in fascination, while she'd be sat at her dressing table in a pale pink dressing gown with a full girdle and tights on underneath. It was important to her that she presented herself to perfection and she took great pride in her appearance.

'You must always check the back of your hair before you leave the house,' she used to say, showing me how to position the mirror so I wouldn't miss a hair out of place. She was pretty skilled in applying makeup, and also taught me how to do it properly, even if there was only a lipstick to hand. 'You pop the lipstick on your lips, then you place a finger onto your lips to gently pick some of the paint up. Dab onto your cheekbone and rub in, giving yourself some colour, just enough to look healthy.' I've used that tip more times than you can imagine!

Gran taught me so much during my time of living with her. I would observe her daily routine and learn a mountain of skills that some people wouldn't learn in a lifetime. Preparing tea and leaving it on the stove; handwashing the laundry then boiling it on the stove; using the twin tub to drain and spin. She'd enjoy a mug of Mellow Bird's coffee while doing the crossword in the Daily Express at the kitchen table, a bowl of bran flakes covered with boiling water in front of her. She polished and hoovered every day, and that was all done before heading into town to meet up with her friends.

She didn't own an ironing board and would iron each day on the kitchen worktop. But one thing Gran taught me during that time that will always be poignant and benefits my life today was how to sew. I bought a long, fitted dress with buttons down the front and it needed taking up as it was far too long. Gran lay a cloth on the worktop, along with the iron, and then showed me how to cut off the excess fabric and complete a double hem that she then taught me how to finish by hand stitching it. It was perfect, and was the start of my sewing journey, though perhaps at the time I didn't realise how significant buying that too-long dress was going to be to my future.

I remember coming in from college one day in my usual casual clothes, this particular time a pair of ripped grey jeans and an old sweater that had seen better days. As I walked through the back door she stopped what she was doing and stared at me up and down with a look of utter disgust. 'Lucy,' she said, 'you look like a bloody orphan!' Never again did I leave my gran's house dressed like that!

After Gran passed away in 2020, I took possession of her beautiful engagement ring, a heavy 18ct white gold band with two diamonds on either side of a dark blue sapphire. But she didn't only leave me that, she also left me two stunning silver bracelets, each one filled with a momentous collection of individual charms. These two pieces of jewellery were especially poignant to Gran's life because she'd collected each charm throughout her years of being a performer. Silver fishes, a 21st key, a swan, a lifeboat, were just some amongst the twenty-six charms that had been lovingly attached to the bracelet's chains, and every single one meant something to my gran. With the bracelets, she'd left a note in her exquisite italic-style handwriting which read:

<u>Small Bracelet:</u>
Original for my 21st; Fishes, Swan, 21st Key, Lifeboat
The rest representing shows I've been in: Indian Rosemary, Pink Champagne, etc.

I was also gifted with a box containing a selection of her diaries, all handwritten of course, and dating back to 1975. I often sit on my own and take out these diaries and read through them. I've done that so many times; it makes me feel serene and takes me back to when the world was buzzing with simplicity and laughter, and I imagine myself being on stage with Gran as she bowed for her audience holding bouquets of flowers, whilst they repeatedly shouted, 'Encore!'

Gran made a firm decision before she passed away and instructed all of us that she didn't want a eulogy written for her at her funeral. It wasn't who she was. Being remembered as a colourful character was how she preferred to be, not an old woman who'd sadly lost her life and therefore the never-ending zest for living. She certainly was a colourful character in many ways, but she was the most fun-loving woman to be around. We all understood why she'd insisted this to be the case when the day finally arrived for us to pay our last respects. She'd even pre-chosen a song to be played at the funeral: *Can't Stop Loving You* by Ray Charles, and at the end, when tears had flowed and we'd all imagined her large as life entering the gates of Heaven, we played at her request, *I Believe* by Robson & Jerome. Then the tears came again. What a beautiful song that is.

The thing was, even though she was adamant that we didn't write our own eulogy, she had actually sent me several pages some years previously that contained enough information about her life to write a book of her own. Here are a few snippets for you to read:

> *I was born at the schoolhouse in 1925. I can remember toddling into school. The headmistress used to let me play with her dog that she brought in ...*
>
> *When I was 11 years old, I went on to the Central School up Leicester Street. The boys*

were on the opposite side of the school. We left school at 3.40pm, the boys left at 4pm. We weren't allowed to mix with them ...

When I was 14, I got home from school one day and my mother said I was to go to Francis's tomorrow to have an interview for a job in the Millinery Dept. I met Mr Francis and he said, "Do you think you'll get any taller, as showroom girls have to be 3'5" upwards?" But instead of making hats, I ended up making sand bags as the war had broken out and they needed to put the bags around the shop ...

At 17, I was called up. I had the choice of Lockheed or the army—I chose Lockheed and I never left home and I was a bit scared ... A man came to me after I'd been there for six weeks from the London offices and said, "I hear you sing. There's a small part in the Pantomime. Would you take it?" I was very thrilled. I can remember singing Shine Through My Dreams. From then on, I went into their concert party and was 'Principal Boy' in pantos for four years ...

We went all over the country singing to troops in army camps. I broadcast from Stoneleigh Army Camp. No such thing as TV then ...

I married when I was 23 years and had 4 lovely sons. While living in Broadway, I had 4 guide dog puppies ...

I went into Leamington and Warwick Operatic Society for 19 years. We had super shows at the Pavilion in Jephson Gardens. I managed the café next door for a short while ...

Lucy Picksley

I re-married a wonderful husband, Vic, at Kenilworth Methodist Church in 1971. We held a reception at The Sycamores Café where we met, a lovely 3-course hot meal for 45 friends - £19.90 the lot ...

I had a step-daughter in Canada, so we often went over there ... walking around Niagara Falls, a wonderful sight ... Sadly my dear husband passed away; I miss him so much. Years later I went to live with Jim. I don't know what I'd do without him, he drives me everywhere and we spend most of our weekends at the RNC ...

I forgot to say that Maria Anderson, the soprano often seen on TV, took me out to dinner at an Italian restaurant with her husband and her manager after singing at the Spa Centre ... Now an old girl at 87 years, I ache all over, can't sing, can't dance, and have a job to walk. But looking back, I've had a good life. Thank you, God.

Some of Gran's diary entries leave me feeling very emotional every time I read them, one in particular where she writes in February 1990 that Vic, her husband, had been admitted to hospital for surgery on his face and this seemed to me that it was probably the start of his decline health-wise. By August, she had written often of his poorly condition, recording whenever the doctor went to visit. And by the last week of that month, she mentions how he was again admitted to hospital, this time saying, *"Vic very ill with prostate ..."*

In September she writes that he is very poorly, though is at home now, and it's quite clear that her life has become considerably stressful as she says, *"A quick dash to get wool then home. Feeling ghastly."* Then, just two days' later, he is taken back to hospital and, according to Gran, *"Drugged up to the hilt."* She ends that diary entry with, *"I want him home."*

By the end of October, she was perhaps accepting that her beloved Vic was only getting worse as she wrote, *"Vic desperately ill, not long now."* It's always so incredibly sad to read, especially as it's been written by someone who was so full of life and then appeared so full of grief.

He passed away on 1st November 1990, and she wrote, *"Vic passed away at 3am. Terrible."* Then she goes on to write about how her heart is broken and how much she continues to miss him. She never stopped writing about him throughout the rest of her life, including an entry in her diary on 6th December every year that simply reads, *"My Vic's birthday."*

Along with this handwritten "autobiography", she'd also written a very personal letter addressed to *My Darling Lucy* ...

> *"How do I start? You brought tears to my eyes when I read your lovely card. It was so lovely to see you again. You're always in my thoughts as I often think of the years you lived with Vic and I at Gresham Avenue. {Gran was confused when she wrote this letter as Vic had already passed away when I moved in with her.} Two of the best people in my life. It would be nice if*

we lived a little nearer so I saw you more often. On the Sunday, it really made my weekend at The Abbey. I still talk to my friends about it. It took me back when I used to entertain the troops with the Concert Party and Broadcast from Stoneleigh Army Camp during the war ..."

You get a feel for my gran just by reading these documents, and you can almost envision her standing before you, enthusiastic and raring to go, having no regrets as she looks back on her wonderfully fascinating life with such exuberance. I've always tended to be a shy person, not someone who throws herself in front of an audience or feels comfortable performing on a stage to a round of applause and the piercing whistles of soldiers. But by July 2022, I think it perhaps came to light that I was more like Gran than I'd ever realised, as a dream came true for me, too, which I will share with you in a future chapter ...

Then, in August of 2022, I took that quilt out of the cupboard, bundled it in the car, and took it to West Whitton in the Yorkshire Dales where we spent a few days on a family holiday. During that time, I finally came to terms with Gran's passing, accepting that she was no longer suffering, and that I'd always have such fond memories of her through not only the quilt, but *Betty*, the Featherweight 221 sewing machine, too.

Elizabeth Marjorie Horswood
"Betty"
11th March 1925 — 3rd January 2020

Chapter Fifteen

As a family, we made a decision to prioritise my university work during the Covid lockdowns as it was imperative that students learnt from patients how healthcare was about to change for everyone. In a household of four, it felt like between the hours of nine-to-five, I was the only one with rules and routines to abide by whilst everyone else got to play games, watch films, and bake. The end of the day would come soon, though, and it was then that I would fall back against the sofa cushions and relax with the family, or seek refuge in my beautiful sewing room ...
"Haven"

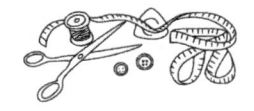

None of us can truly talk about the Covid pandemic with fondness. It was an awful time and for some, it was the worst time of their lives. The world became a very small place within a matter of weeks as countries closed their borders and we had to live like hermits, with the fear of God should we wish to venture outside for a five-minute break or a bit of fresh air. So many people made the world continue to function as best as it could, so many who didn't get a mention or acknowledgement for their wonderful efforts and commitments. We all know who they are, we all have someone, be a loved one or a friend, or a group of people whom we will always be immensely grateful to for allowing us at least a grain of freedom in what felt like being trapped in a broken down lift.

Areas all around the country became ghost-towns and public buildings such as leisure centres, pubs, shops and hostelries closed their doors, many unable to survive the course due to a lack of profit. There was a significant lack of cars on the roads and we had that image of an apocalyptic world in our heads. Tumbleweed rolling across a deserted carriageway with a whistling gale blowing eerily in the distance.

Family time became important for all of us as socialising with friends was now out of the question. Mark's business came to a standstill. He's the director of a community interest company that collect and redistribute furniture back into the community. He hires volunteers who have been out of work for lengthy periods and helps them get back into the world of employment by giving them a few hours of work each week to enable them to feel part of something again. Whilst working with Mark, they then start to feel valuable, needed, a part of the community, and it gives them a huge sense of purpose. When we went into lockdown, Mark had to stay at home so these people were no longer able to volunteer or work. The company wasn't regarded as "essential" or its employees as "key workers" and so Mark ended up being a kind of house-husband where he took over the main responsibilities of caring for the boys and looking after the household chores.

Education establishments also closed their doors, which meant I started to work from home. It was a few weeks after we'd gone into the first lockdown, when everyone was anxious and having no clue about this new way of life we were all expected to adhere to, that I received a phone call from a technician in the School of Fashion, one of the schools within the university. She'd been given my name by a colleague and wanted to talk to me, after being told I was a proficient and fast sewist, about making scrubs for the hospitals. It was no secret that the NHS was struggling. PPE was taking too long to be delivered and the whole concept of needing more and more supplies to meet the extensive demands was at breaking point. The time had come when skilled seamsters were being called upon to help out. This had become an emergency situation, and it simply couldn't go on the way it was. I was more than happy to assist as I'm very much involved with "community action" and understand the need for communities to merge and work together. To give you a little idea of community action, it is about understanding the needs of neighbourhoods and working with people to mobilise and take charge. I used to run a sewing group one evening per month with The Sew Social Club, and we'd made items to give out to the community, one being knitted hats for babies. This work gave me a great deal of pride, as it enabled funding to be provided to high deprivation areas in order to improve much-needed facilities. It was exhausting, I can't lie, and it put my skills to the utmost test sometimes, it also drove me round the bend occasionally, but it was all worth it in the end.

The sense of achievement the community action gave me was a massive boost to my confidence and self-esteem, but when the technician at the School of Fashion expressed how much they needed me to be a part of the team, a small select group of sewists to contribute vital items to help the NHS through what was proving probably their biggest challenge to date, I felt epic.

I set off along the A156 on the day they wanted me to start, making my way towards the university. The roads were hauntingly quiet, so few cars about, just the odd lorry and supermarket delivery vans, and they were scarce. I drove onto campus and it was the strangest feeling to see hardly any cars in the car park and dozens of spaces free, something quite out of the ordinary when it would normally take me ages to find a spot. I parked up and made my way inside where Fiona, the technician, was waiting to greet me. No handshaking or getting too close; we stood two metres apart with our facemasks on and I followed her into the hall where huge boards had been set out, displaying plans and indicating instructions and requests on how we would move this huge project forward.

For the Love of Lincolnshire Scrubs Team—that was our group name. There were rolls and rolls of fabric laid out and we were asked who would prefer to work from home and who on campus. Lists had to be made for those people who wanted their materials to be delivered to their homes, and I remember a lady, though I can't recall her name, who would ride miles and miles on her bike each day to deliver parcels to home-workers, collecting their completions to take back to the university and be distributed as and when. I imagine that lady did an average of forty miles a day riding around Lincolnshire!

The task I was given was to cut up to six layers of fabric in batches, different sizes and shapes to make items such as tunics and trousers. I still dream about the amount of pockets, facings and sleeves I cut over those weeks; in fact, so many that my scissors came to the end of their natural life! The work was demanding and tiring and would leave us exhausted by the end of the day. But it was also difficult as we'd hear countless stories about staff on the hospital wards who were at breaking point, struggling to cope with the endless admissions, and in some cases unable to concentrate for the whole of their shifts. It really was a dire situation for many of them and I'd say with confidence that unless you were in that position and seeing it all happening first hand yourself, it would be quite difficult to grasp the enormity of how stressed these professional medical staff really were.

What we were doing to help wasn't like sewing as I knew it; there was nothing therapeutic or enjoyable. The rewards were, of course, worth it, because we knew we were helping so many people, but the demands on us were extreme. Our group consisted of a great bunch of people, though, and we'd chat and get to know each other.

The items that we made weren't individual sizes but were made in XS, S, M, L, XL, etc. The fabric used was donated by individuals, shops and warehouses, not purchased or funded by the NHS or the government, and these donors would make contact with the community group that had been up in their area in order to offer their materials. The fabrics that we received were donated by Lincoln University. A Facebook group had been set up called *For the Love of Scrubs*, and administrators posted geographical areas and encouraged members to set up their own groups within those areas. The page for the county of Lincolnshire was so inspiring, grabbing the attention of huge amounts of people and really encouraging them to engage in this wonderful community spirit. People from all over were working in their homes, cutting and sewing and providing scrubs for hospitals all over the country. Even novice seamsters, beginners and those who perhaps hadn't sewn anything in their lives were keen to get onboard. Facemasks were an easy item to make and many of the novices would get to work and create these, leaving the more complicated tunics and trousers to the more experienced amongst us. But the way everyone came together was something I was extremely proud to be a part of.

On a daily basis, requests were flooding in for new sets of scrubs and we were working round the clock to try and meet demand. The problem was that fabrics and materials were starting to dry up and we got to a point where every piece, every centimetre of elastic for the elasticated waists on trousers and masks, had to be accounted for. Eventually, we had to reduce the amount of pockets on garments, and that ended up being reduced yet again to none at all. We needed to preserve fabric and not use any unnecessarily.

At the start of the project, I guess we felt a buzz knowing that our efforts were going to hospital staff who were helping people in crisis, those trapped in Covid wards and being rushed in for emergency treatment. Children's wards were also demanding items and from home, I made two sets of *My Little Pony* scrubs and a set of *Thomas the Tank Engine* ones, which I fashioned for Haydn as he was a massive Thomas fan. I imagined the children's faces as nurses wandered the wards wearing those outfits. A simple, tiny bit of pleasure that would hopefully light up a little one's face and make them smile, if just for a short while. I also made a special set for a doctor who was really starting to struggle and I was told needed something to help him get through—lift his spirits and make his job just a smidgen easier. And so I made him a set of beautiful orange scrubs in a quality cotton fabric, and added a matching drawstring bag with a navy pull that I placed them in. He was delighted.

Whilst all this was going on, and when I eventually got home from a long day making scrubs, I would hide away in the studio for a bit, and focus my attention on a creation I'd wanted to work on for some time: my own jeans, made from scratch. I had intended enrolling on a course to learn how to make them but because courses had become a thing of the past and we didn't know when life would get back to normal again, I chose those months during Covid to give myself enough time and space to fulfil this ambition on my own.

As the months progressed, resources dwindled and we were beyond tired. The pressure we were all under was something I'd never experienced in my sewing career. Something I will always remember during that difficult time was how our little team would spend lunch breaks on the terrace, standing apart from each other, quietly eating our sandwiches. I would put my head back and allow the sun's rays to hit my face as I closed my eyes and wondered what the future held.

Chapter Sixteen

Visiting Granddad Sid was always a pleasure, although his gas fire hit you with the heat it kicked off whatever time of year. He didn't have much to say really, just news about his crown green bowling and a bit of a giggle about his women woes! From there, we would visit Aunty Hilda, where she'd usually be outside in her garden, digging up her supper. She would usher us into the kitchen where she would give her fork and spade a quick wash, before popping the kettle on to boil. She would then go to her sideboard and pull out a bag of sweets, inviting us to help ourselves, though would tell us off if we dared take more than one ...

"Stonehouse"

Sue, a very dear friend of mine, first introduced herself to me by making an enquiry about me teaching her how to sew. She was particularly interested in making a "tea dress", with a full circle skirt. It was a difficult make for a beginner, but with my help, we were sure that between us we could do it justice. We spent hours drinking tea and chatting, having a great laugh as we put that dress together, and before long those days of me teaching Sue the skills of sewing materialised into spending full days in each other's company. Our friendship blossomed, we had such a lot in common, because we both adored anything craft related. It eventually came about that in exchange for me helping Sue how to make her dress and other garments, she started teaching me how to do block printing and how to marble fabrics. It was an arrangement that worked for both of us, not only because we were coming up with all sorts of fancy designs, but also because we thoroughly enjoyed spending time together. Sue couldn't care less about splashing paint all over her table at home, or me doing it, for that matter; just as long as we were having fun, that was all she cared about.

Sue's elderly mother lived in a purpose-built annexe, or granny flat, as some call it, attached to their family home, and this meant Sue was always on hand to help should her mother need it. She was known to everyone as Nanna Rose, and so that's what I called her, too. It was perhaps inevitable that one day Sue would need to be there more for her mother, but she never complained. She would have done anything to help and indeed, as Nanna Rose got older, Sue dedicated many hours to looking after her.

Sue mentioned to me one day that even though her mother, who was now in a wheelchair, was ageing and now in her 90s, she still wanted to look good, taking pride in her appearance and felt the need to stay young-minded. She wanted to feel wonderful and comfortable in her clothes, and so I had a chat with Nanna Rose and she told me quite determinedly that she loved wearing dresses. The only problem she had, she went on to say, was that whenever she wore one while sat in her wheelchair, they rose to above the knee and she didn't feel comfortable, but if she wore a much longer dress, it wasn't something she liked and had a tendency to get caught in the wheels of her chair. And so, after a chat with Sue, it was decided that I would make her mother a few suitable dresses that would hopefully make her feel good again and would be something she'd enjoy wearing. Sue's suggestion was to use gentle fabrics with a finish that wouldn't rub against Nanna Rose's skin, designed so they were easy to get on and off. We did some research and found just what we needed and it wasn't long until Sue's mother had a small selection of dresses in what had now become partly a handmade wardrobe. One of the dresses was made of soft-touch jersey fabric in pale blue and had subtle white lines running through it. I always smile when I remember her face as she tried that dress on. She adored it and it looked beautiful on her. Its long sleeves fitted perfectly to just above her wrists, and she wore a string of pearls around her neck when she put it on, adding to the look that made her appear regal and proud. It was a simple design but Nanna Rose looked so good in it that she could have been a guest at a Royal Garden Party and completely fit in.

The next dress she tried on was again a jersey fabric, but with a boat neck and shorter sleeves that rested just above her elbows. Pink, lilac, and green flowers nestled elegantly against a navy-blue background, which made Nanna Rose look years younger. Her smile once again beamed from ear-to-ear as she posed for a photograph, delighted at how smart she looked. Another dress in this collection was a pale blue background, again with a flowery design, this time in different shades of pink with browns mixed in. It had darts to the front and back and a full skirt to the bottom.

Hummingbirds and Kaleidoscopes

But one of her favourite dresses was one I'd made often, and I have to admit it was my favourite, too. It's called the Bertine dress by Tilly and the Buttons. Made of a soft cotton fabric, it had a navy-blue background with large, white polka dots that really brought out the striking effect. With an attractive scoop neck and an adequate drape to offer comfort, it rested at just the right length for Nanna Rose's taste below the knee and not too far down the shin. It also had two deep pockets at the front that she would be able to keep tissues in.

Lovely Nanna Rose, with the huge grin and kind heart, sadly passed away at the age of ninety-two, just a few months after I'd made the polka-dot dress. It was very sad to hear, of course, and naturally upsetting for Sue. But something that warmed my heart after her passing was when Sue told me that her mother had been cremated in that very same polka-dot dress, and even though Sue said she'd felt terrible about it, I was incredibly touched. Nanna Rose had felt comfortable in the dress and adored it, and she would now begin her next journey in both comfort and style, wearing a dress I had lovingly made for her. To imagine this dear elderly lady walking through the pearly gates looking as beautiful as she did whilst wearing that dress, meant the world to me, and it always will. God Bless you, Nanna Rose.

A lovely man called Simon approached me for sewing lessons, and this was another project that really lifted my spirits. You see, Simon has a serious health condition known as Acute Lymphoblastic Leukaemia, which caused extensive damage to his heart, lungs, liver, and pancreas. It means he needs to constantly use an oxygen tank at home, as well as a portable one, which he carries around whenever he leaves the house. Quite debilitating for him, as I'm sure you can imagine. Not only did the oxygen tank draw attention, but it was quite a cumbersome piece of equipment that he preferred people didn't stare at. And so, with the intention of making a bag to cover the portable tank up with, he asked for my help.

For the purpose of this book, I asked Simon a few questions and his answers, below, left me feeling somewhat humble, yet proud of being able to assist him with this project. Suffice to say, he got a lot out of our time sewing together, as did I …

> *Making the bag was a really pleasurable experience. It was made based on a previous pattern of Lucy's. I loved the way it slowly came together and the fact this would be part of me and had a very meaningful purpose. I loved the way we adapted the bag to meet the requirements of the concentrator. For example, incorporating mesh panelling to ensure that the machine could breathe in air to function properly.*
>
> *The way we both worked together was so enjoyable, problem solving each stage and sharing each other's expertise and knowledge. Lucy with her sewing and designing knowledge, and me as an oxygen user, showing her how the machine functioned and its requirements. I think that's what made the process so enjoyable;*

the achievement we both shared and how it came together so successfully. It wasn't just a bag that was going to hang on a clothes peg, but something I would benefit from and admire each day.

I love the design of the bag. The primary material used is Oil Cloth, which was suggested by Lucy to give it that strong masculine look, with Kaffe Fassett lining. The way the bag aesthetically looks is amazing (non-clinical). I can walk around and almost feel and look normal. Something I feel more happier and confident wearing, not forgetting how proud I am of the whole journey of its design and production.

The feedback from friends and family has been shock, basically from the achievement in such a short period of time sewing. Once over the shock they have been really impressed with its purpose and functionality. I have been approached by a few people (public) that have understood what it actually is, and they have loved it. I believe they think it was originally purchased, but I love explaining that I made it with my sewing teacher.

There are so many reasons I sew with Lucy. She became a sewing friend rather than a teacher and I am sure that made the process of learning far easier and more enjoyable. The achievement and knowledge I have obtained from lessons in such a short period of time is phenomenal. When things don't go to plan, it's fun and enjoyable to rectify. Lucy is very accommodating with my health limitations and very understanding, even though she has very little knowledge of my health issues, and to me that's very important and reassuring. Simon.

Chapter Seventeen

I love how fashion trends roll around over time, coming back with a bang or to haunt us all over again. It's a bit like music. On my son's playlist I hear some of my all-time favourites being ripped to pieces as they are reworked for a younger, more modern audience. If you'd told me that Kate Bush would be Running Up that Hill in 2023, I would have called you bonkers …
"Exham"

It was autumn 2021 when a lady called Karen contacted me after she'd been researching sewing tutors on Google. She wasn't confident that she could learn or whether I could teach her, but she was enthusiastic and had been experimenting a little at home with her own sewing machine. She'd made a drawstring bag, but admitted it wasn't great and decided it was time to reach out for help. One thing that Karen did point out to me on her first communication was that she is left-handed, which can create issues if you don't have the right equipment. Most patterns and instructions are aimed at right-handed sewists, and when it comes to using scissors to cut fabric, this is also a challenge unless you have acquired a pair of left-handed ones. I've always liked a bit of problem solving, and so I was keen to help her, responding to her email by telling her that I could help, and inviting her to my home studio.

She arrived shortly after and I welcomed her in, as did my four rather curious cats. Unfortunately, Karen was absolutely petrified of cats and after reassuring her they were completely harmless, she simply couldn't shake off the phobia she had, even if one just looked at her. I didn't want my feline friends to put her off coming back and so we arranged that she would knock on the front door in future rather than go through the gate to my studio, then have to step back three metres, allowing me time to open the door and shoo the cats from sight. This seemed to help and she felt a lot happier about future visits.

We got on well right from the outset. A lovely, kind lady with eight children, three of which were grown up by then, and five of whom she home-schooled, she opened up to me quite soon after we first met and told me how she'd fled an abusive relationship twenty years previously and moved from the South East to a refuge in Lincolnshire. I didn't expect her to elaborate on what she'd been through, I imagined it would have been too traumatic to talk about, and as it had happened two decades ago, I guess she'd put it all behind her anyway. But at the time, her three daughters were just nine, five, and two years old respectively, and she did enlighten me on some of the emotional aspects it had on her children. She'd been looked after, along with her girls, and been able to start a new life in a new county. She found herself happy again in a relationship and went on to have another five children.

Apart from being a good person, Karen, along with her eldest daughter, wanted to give something back, to help other children and adults who end up in the same or a similar situation as theirs, and that was when she decided to start making the drawstring bags. The idea of the bag was to fill it with a teddy bear, a drawing book or a note book, and a set of stationery. It was important to Karen to begin this project and it made me quite proud to know she'd chosen me to help her improve her skills in making the bags. She had devised meanings behind each item that would be included in the bag and I found this to be particularly endearing. The bear would be to provide emotional support to a child; the book and stationery would be used to create, draw, imagine, and record special memories or activities that had been carried out with a caregiver, parent, or someone who would be assigned to help them after the upheaval of fleeing abusive homes. The whole concept provided a really positive outcome and I knew when I started teaching Karen that first day that she was destined for good things to happen.

Karen's first intention when she began her sewing journey was to improve her bag-making skills, to create something simple that would look professional and not be quite so complicated to make. She also wanted to make a teddy bear, but we soon established that it was more important at that stage to enhance her sewing creations and make bags that would stand the test of time. And so, we set to work and made her first, simple drawstring bag. It was made from a red fabric with white stars on it and had a red pull cord. It was a simple design, but Karen was proud of it, as was I. This encouraged her to go to the next step and make rucksack-type bags, which would be used for older children. The first of these bags Karen made as a pair, and she was so proud of her achievement that she kept one of them for herself as a keepsake to remind her of how far she had come since fleeing all those years ago and learning to live again. Her face beamed with delight as she admired her own work, part of her unable to believe she had actually created these beautiful designs.

Suffice to say, she came to my studio every week and her sewing went from strength to strength, making items including a sewing machine cover, a pencil case, and a caddy which she keeps fabrics in. She also made a "project" bag for one of her sons along with quite an extravagant bag to keep her knitting in. She also went on to make her youngest daughter a smock top and leggings to match, something she wore with pride.

Karen not only spent her time sewing and making clothes and other items for her family, but she also home-schooled her five younger children. Her days were completely filled from morning till night and one couldn't help but admire her zest for life, especially after what she'd been through. Her home sewing machine was quite problematic and she invited me to her house one day in the hope I would be able to help her use it more effectively. We sat at her kitchen table where her own materials surrounded her and this gave me a better understanding of how she worked as a sewist. It was during this visit that I met her children—three girls and two boys, aged between eight and fifteen—all with their own personalities and interests. I found this fascinating because Karen's youngest child was chatty and had a fun character, whilst her eldest (of the five from her new relationship), Meghan, sat at the table and quietly observed us, watching her mum use the sewing machine and listening to me giving her tips and advice. She seemed interested in what we were doing and after a while began to open up a little, telling me about her own creations and offering to show me. I, of course, jumped at this opportunity and was very impressed with the girl's designs. Something I did notice was that she had similar traits to Brady, being quiet and coming across as somewhat introvert, yet just wanting the chance to talk to someone, share things with, and perhaps learn new skills. Karen had already told me about her concerns for Meghan, and added how she often found it difficult to give her the support she needed, not really knowing where to go for that support or if indeed there was any available. After what I'd been through myself with Brady, I knew there was help out there but it was a battle to access and would mean a lot of assessments, appointments, and meetings with the local authority.

I shared some of my own experiences with Karen that day, telling her about the difficulties we'd had over the years and how challenging our lives had been for various reasons, and adding that I would provide her with online resources and places she could turn to in order to hopefully get the help Meghan needed. I was especially pleased when Karen later told me that the advice I'd given her was invaluable and her daughter did her own research and shared her findings with Karen. This ultimately led to their mother-daughter relationship being so much more bonded, and it is also with thanks to Brady that this is the case because he, too, provided his own information having gone through it first-hand, to both Karen and Meghan.

I mentioned my love of Sashiko to Karen and explained how it was an easy process to teach, and was especially simple for children to learn. Using items such as a needle, thread, fabric, stencil and chalk makes it low risk of injury, of course with supervision if children are involved. But she was happy for me to show her five children this skill and we arranged for me to go back to her house and show them this very beautiful method of sewing. I remember her youngest daughter, the one who'd been chatty and funny on my first visit when we sat at the kitchen table trying to fathom out Karen's sewing machine, was very keen to learn, but after about half an hour she got frustrated, spending most of her time fighting with the thread. Sashiko is an activity each child could learn at their own pace, but I guess it isn't for everyone! The two boys, aged nine and eleven, immersed themselves in it and seemed to thoroughly enjoy the time I spent showing them how to stitch. Karen told me they'd even carried on after I left, and David*, the nine-year-old, was completely focused, carrying on his new-found hobby and sewing many more designs. The other two girls also enjoyed the process and went on to create some beautiful designs in their own time.

As Karen got more and more into her sewing, along with her daughter Meghan, she announced one day that she wanted to learn how to crochet. The only issue where that was concerned was the fact she's left-handed and I'm right-handed, as this would prove more challenging than it would normally. I'd never held a crochet needle in my left hand and so teaching her this skill wasn't going to be easy. However, me being me, I was willing to accept the challenge and told her I was confident I could help.

It was a shame some thirty minutes' later when I had to admit defeat. Right-handed I might be; ambidextrous I am not! Though a very positive occurrence took place as a result of me not being able to teach Karen how to crochet, as Meghan took it upon herself to learn also, and wanting to help her mum, she then taught herself how to do it left-handed. What an incredibly wonderful thing for a daughter to do, I thought, as I saw how much this delighted Karen, encouraging them both to sit down together and take up this hobby like two close friends. Karen now felt inspired, knowing the help she needed to learn was right there, beside her.

But above all of this, and what has been the most amazing thing to come from Karen's willingness to learn, is that she has since created her own charity, officially set up in its own right. She and her eldest daughter apply their skills to make drawstring bags and rucksacks, containing Karen's initial idea of a teddy bear, a colouring book or a notebook, and a set of stationery, then hand them out to children who have been pronounced temporarily homeless due to domestic abuse and having to escape their homes. The charity, known as "Journey, With Love" has become hugely successful and gone on to help many families in crisis.

The biggest and most prominent area in which I helped Karen to improve was by far overcoming her fear of just getting on with the job of sewing; starting that first drawstring bag and learning how to use the sewing machine properly. I removed that fear she had of cutting fabric and using lots of different colours and materials. We all make mistakes throughout our professional career and it's often very much a learning curve. But Karen acknowledged her mistakes and tackled them head on. I encouraged her from that first lesson when she arrived at the studio, terrified of four sets of feline eyes watching her every move, that it was okay not to be perfect; that we learn as we go along and we do it at our own pace.

I am so proud of Karen, and of course Siobhan, and feel privileged to have met these two very inspirational people and to have been able to pass on my own sewing skills to enable them to help so many women and children in need. Karen recently wrote to me with the following words, which I will always treasure:

> *I think the mental health side and connection with sewing, and working with you specifically, worked so well because of your openness and natural curiosity in people and their lives. I feel safe with you.*

*Name changed to protect privacy

Chapter Eighteen

For the past few years, Mark and I have travelled to Nottingham to see their winter wonderland and enjoy the buzz that exudes from the streets lined in pretty little chalet huts, highly decorated in lights and tinsel. It's not the shopping that I love so much, but the atmosphere. The chance to stop and stare, watch the world go by through the eyes of a small child who has shaken their snow globe and is watching flakes float in the air with all the joy, magic, and hope that Christmas brings…
"Market Day"

It was spring 2021 and Brady was fifteen. He'd been seeing a girl of the same age for a while, a light-hearted friendship that Mark and I were comfortable with him having. Suzie would come to our house and have tea, and we'd take her with us on family days' out, where we'd watch them together, happy and enjoying each other's company. It was young love, and perhaps his first experience of having a special person in his life other than the family, who he could care about and spend time with, laughing and chatting about the same things. I sometimes thought it might have been a bit intense for two teenagers as we could clearly see it was more than just a friendship, i.e., two mates getting together outside school. But seeing our eldest boy smiling and enjoying himself meant too much to Mark and I to start laying down rules; we were just relieved that he seemed to be happy.

When his relationship with Suzie came to a natural end, he was of course upset, and I talked to him and consoled him, making sure he didn't take it too badly. Fortunately, he got over it by himself and before long started spending time with Zoe, just as friends at first, but we could see there was more to it and it was obvious Brady was smitten with her. When they moved their friendship on and became girlfriend and boyfriend, it felt quite different to the relationship he'd had with Suzie. Zoe was shy and a little reserved and she preferred to meet Brady away from home. We respected that and didn't interfere in how they conducted themselves. They'd go for long walks together and would hang out in social spaces, listening to music and just being by themselves as they watched the world go by. It was obvious from early on that there was a deep love between them, though it was also noticeable that the feelings were more intense from Brady's point of view.

He would have walked to the moon and back for this girl; his emotions were very much focused on her. Looking back in hindsight, we could see that he had become obsessed with her and we knew it was perhaps somewhat unhealthy at his young and impressionable age. But again, he was happy, and we'd been through so much with him in previous years that we just wanted to see him smile, to enjoy his life as he deserved to, and have someone in his life he could enjoy spending time with.

They would message each other constantly on their mobile phones and the moment she said she was ready to go out, he would head over to her house. She would also suggest meeting up the following day, but with no clear indication of when or where, and this would never sit well with Brady. His condition needs routine, planning, stability, or he becomes restless and anxious and unable to deal with the everyday regularities that you and I wouldn't give a second thought to. He would get up early, with the understanding they were meeting up, he'd have a shower and get dressed, then sit on his bed wearing his coat and shoes and wait for Zoe to message him again, giving him a time to collect her or a place where they could meet. He would wait for hours sometimes, staring at his phone, scared to put it down in case he missed her message. And to our irritation, it seemed to be happening more and more that she would change plans on the last minute, or tell him she couldn't make that day after all. As his mum, it hurt me terribly to see Brady come out of his room, a look of absolute devastation on his face, mixed with confusion and heartbreak, only to tell me he wasn't going out as Zoe couldn't make it. Because of his feelings towards her, Mark and I noticed his anxiety levels were beginning to rise again, which concerned us, especially after he'd seemed so happy with his new girlfriend. He was hurting and it showed in his expression and his mannerisms. And that, in turn, was awful to witness.

But Brady didn't blame Zoe for changing their plans or cancelling a date, or just rearranging the time they'd agreed to meet up. He was too besotted with her to put any blame on her because he would have felt he was doing wrong by her. He saw her through loyal eyes, an unconditional adoration that we suspected by now was one way. Then, when she'd finally message him to say she was ready, he'd dash from the house and race to meet her. She lived a few miles away and he would run there, sometimes to find she'd already left her house and hadn't left any indication as to where she might be. Not knowing where to look for her, he'd then walk home again, upset and distressed at the fact she'd stood him up, and his emotions would come crashing down to earth with a massive bump.

We had decided to let him get on with the relationship as we were well aware of how shy Zoe appeared to be and the fact Brady wanted to get to know her on his own without his parents inviting her round for Sunday dinner every week and bombarding her with questions. It had started off well as far as we were concerned, but we were quickly coming to the conclusion that this relationship wasn't all it was cracked up to be. Mark and I were naturally curious about them both, and had to remind ourselves often that we were young once, carefree and wanting to be alone with a boyfriend or girlfriend. That to have parents wanting to know our every move would have been a complete nightmare. And so we adopted this concept with Brady, wanting to allow him to accept responsibility and learn for himself about the nature of being with someone.

The tide began to turn late spring when he got into the habit of leaving the house late evening, telling us he "needed" to see Zoe. It was as though he was desperate to be with her and when we'd ask why he needed to leave so late, he didn't really have an answer. He just felt he should go to her, but was unable to understand why. At fifteen, we knew we had to tread carefully because he was in that age range of being classed as a "young adult", but these nights of him feeling he *had* to leave the house and be with Zoe were making his behaviour erratic and we noticed he seemed fearful about something. Perhaps about never seeing her again, about her finishing their relationship, about her being with someone else. It didn't make enough sense to us and even though we tried to talk to him and suggest that surely she could wait until tomorrow, he wasn't prepared to listen and would argue that Zoe needed him and that he must go, as though he had little choice in the matter. To prevent further anxiety and any arguments and meltdowns, we'd watch him leave and would wait for a message or a phone call sometime later for us to pick him up. Sometimes, that would be after midnight and into the early hours.

It was about ten-to-twelve one night when my mobile phone rang. I was in bed and the shrill of the ring tone woke me up immediately. The person on the other end of the phone was Mr Quince, Head of Safeguarding at Brady's school.

'Mrs Picksley?' he said.

'Yes, speaking ...'

'Are you aware that Brady isn't at home?'

I sat up straight in bed, my heart now thumping heavy in my chest as Mark lay next to me. 'Sorry? I'm not sure what you mean,' I replied, totally dazed and confused.

'I've received an email from Brady telling me he's in distress.'

My reaction was nothing short of being dumbfounded as I threw the duvet off me and ran downstairs to Brady's room, flung open the door and saw that he wasn't there.

We weren't sure when Brady had sent Mr Quince the email, whether or not he'd still been at home when he'd told him he was in distress, but what we then learned was that this incredibly kind man had taken Brady's email so seriously that he'd driven to the school, unlocked the gates, parked up, then unlocked the main entrance and gone to the admin office where pupils' files were kept. He'd taken Brady's file out of the filing cabinet and looked for a phone number to contact either myself or Mark. He was as worried about our son as we were and assured us he would not be going to bed that night until he knew Brady was safe and back at home. The story with Mr Quince didn't end there, as his amazing support extended to all of us as a family and he went on to become Brady's go-to person of contact whenever he needed to talk or found himself in trouble. And even after Brady left secondary school, Mr Quince continued to help him, offering a listening ear and assistance should he ever need it.

As no one knew of Brady's whereabouts on that night that Mr Quince had first contacted us, we felt we had no other option but to call the police and report him missing. The police were on hand straight away, knowing Brady was a vulnerable young person, and they set out in a patrol car, touring around the town and the outskirts, up and down streets and residential areas, until eventually, they spotted him standing alone by the River Trent at around three in the morning. They bundled him in the car and brought him home, and after Mark and I decided it was too late at night now to discuss what he'd done, we promised ourselves we would sit him down the following day and try to make him realise how unacceptable his behaviour was.

Hummingbirds and Kaleidoscopes

By the summer, he was going out most nights, sometimes very late after we'd all gone to bed, and we assumed he was tucked up beneath the duvet. This happened about every two to three nights, and I would wake up with a feeling of dread, knowing he wouldn't be in his room. We live in a three-storey house and I would quietly pad downstairs to his bedroom on the first floor, open his door and see that he had indeed gone. He left me a note one night that told me not to worry, that he'd had to go to Zoe because she needed him, but it was only that one time he did leave a note. All the other times we had to assume he'd gone there, and because he never answered his phone to us, we'd end up being awake wondering what the hell to do. We often rang Zoe's dad to ask if Brady was there, but often her dad would tell us he wasn't, and neither was Zoe. Two fifteen-year-olds out in the middle of the night, wandering around God knows where, was becoming a regular occurrence, and one we were finding increasingly stressful. Zoe's dad, who was a single parent, together with Mark and I, would take it in turns to go out in the car and drive around town, up and down deserted streets where there was no streetlight, hoping and praying we'd see them. I hated being in the car on my own on those nights, lonely and afraid, crying and often sobbing as I'd steer into another side road and find it empty of people, just parked cars and rows of houses with closed curtains at the windows.

Not answering his phone was vexing, because we'd talked so often about how much we worried about him and how irresponsible and unfair it was for him to disappear without letting us know where he was.

Then, one night, he sent me a text message and attached a photo to it of the Trent Bridge. The water was fast-flowing below it and anyone could forgive me for assuming the worst. His behaviour was spiralling out of control and once again we knew we were facing more challenges, only this time from a child much older and perhaps wiser to the concept of doing right from wrong.

I was in constant fear for his safety, imagining him being swept away in a strong current, or lying injured in an alleyway having been attacked. Zoe's father was, of course, very anxious, not to mention losing patience with their antics. His daughter, though we felt was more streetwise than Brady, was still disrespecting her dad, knowing he'd be worried sick about where she was. The pressure Brady put us under during that time was phenomenal. We couldn't get through to him no matter how hard we tried; he didn't want to listen to reason because his only focus was Zoe and what she needed. What Mark and I needed was for our boy to realise what he was doing to our mental health and that we, as his parents, had every right to worry about him.

The stress we were under as a couple was starting to create cracks in our marriage as we knew neither of us were coping well. One of us would stay up as we didn't dare go to bed, hoping to catch Brady and encourage him not to go out. We'd take it in turns to sleep on the sofa, even on the landing near his bedroom, and we'd hide his keys and ours. We were desperate to help him, even though he felt our help wasn't something he required. And despite him having no means of leaving the house through the front door, he took to climbing out of his bedroom window and somehow manoeuvring himself onto the drainpipe, before sliding down it and running away from the house.

His obsession, infatuation, whatever you want to call it, had reached breaking point and the problems we were now facing had got to the stage where we had no more answers. The family were in a permanent state of panic, Haydn was still so young, and eventually we seemed to lose the will to fight what was starting to destroy our unity. We watched our eldest son on a daily basis drift further and further away from us. But when we started noticing cuts on his arms, I couldn't take any more and my doctor signed me off work for a month. My nerves were shattered, I was a quivering wreck, and I'd literally stopped coping again.

The self-harming, unfortunately, became more intense over the next few months and Brady's cuts would extend along both his arms in rows. It was harrowing to see. He had also taken to punching walls, ripping his hands and knuckles to shreds, and would have to have them bandaged up, only to tear the bandages away and start again, reopening the already distressed wounds.

That Christmas, in 2021, was the last time Brady ran off to be with Zoe …

Chapter Nineteen

I knew what GCSE results I needed to get into college, four of them needing to be above a C-grade. When I gained an A in Art, I knew then that I had a thirst for the creative aspects of life and wanted to go to the further education college that was well-regarded for its Arts and Textile Design course. The only problem was, the college was 120 miles south, back in my birthplace of Leamington Spa. Thankfully, I had a wonderful gran who wanted to support me and so for the next two years, I moved my belongings to her house and she took care of me as I made myself at home in her guest bedroom ...
"Clarendon"

If you are aware of self-harming, you will understand how upsetting it is to see your child with injuries they have inflicted upon themselves. It's a way of reaching out for help, sending a message to the world to say you're deeply unhappy, can't control your emotions, that you feel you have little to live for yet know there's something that could perhaps switch on the light at the end of your darkest tunnel. You're feeling such intense pain within your thoughts and your heart, that you need to hurt yourself physically, cause superficial wounds and scars to help you focus on another kind a pain rather than the one you are unable to cope with. Children who self-harm often don't understand their own emotions and can't deal with the world around them as it continues to spin. It's like they feel caught in a net under water, with no means of escape. Children aren't mature enough to shake themselves off and say "tomorrow's another day". They often can't envision "tomorrow", or even the night time of that same day. They're telling whoever is willing to listen that they're not okay, that they need help, support, someone to talk to. Brady's self-harming had got out of control and his distress calls were becoming more and more frequent.

When he made his final visit to Zoe's house, she refused to let him in. She didn't even answer the door. Perhaps her dad had instructed her not to as we knew he'd had enough, just like we had, but we felt she could have at least given him an explanation as to why their relationship came to an abrupt end.

Something Brady hardly ever did was ring Mark or myself to tell us where he was, and this was something that would upset us tremendously. We pleaded with him to just send us a quick message if not a phone call, but he hardly ever did. However, as things were obviously coming to a head with Zoe, just before their relationship ended, Brady did occasionally text me to say he was safe, that he was okay, and that I didn't need to worry. *Ha!* I used to think. *I'm your mum, it's my job to worry!* But I was always grateful of the message and it did put my mind at rest, if only for a short time.

The night that Zoe refused to open the door to Brady, her way of telling him it was over, my mobile phone rang out and his name flashed up on the screen. It was one o'clock in the morning, and I knew in my gut that something had happened. He cried during that phone call, asking me to go and fetch him to bring him home, and that was exactly what I did, without a moment's hesitation. The streets were quiet and there wasn't a soul about, except my boy, standing in a deserted street, crying and utterly bereft. He got into the front passenger seat and put his seatbelt on and I set off, he raised his feet onto the dashboard and started to kick the windscreen until he turned his body towards the passenger window and repeatedly punched it. It was a 60mph-limit road and I drove all the way home doing just 5mph, terrified of the damage he was likely doing not only to my car, but to himself, too. We both cried on that journey home, for different reasons. My son was sat beside me completely heartbroken because his girlfriend had finished with him. I was completely heartbroken because of the state my son was in. Being a parent is so tough, in so many ways. Yet it can also be filled with love and the intensity of never giving up.

When we finally arrived home after that torturous drive back, I went upstairs with Brady and followed him into his bedroom where I helped to clean the wounds he'd self-inflicted upon himself. I filled a hot water bottle for him and switched on his TV, tuning into his favourite episode of Spiderman. Then I sat at the bottom of his bed whilst he made himself comfortable beneath the duvet, and together, after a short time, we fell asleep.

'Every day is a new day,' has always been a mantra I've recited to my boys when they've been upset about something, worrying that the problem might never be solved. Brady knows this means he won't be punished for something that happened yesterday; perhaps it

won't be forgotten for a while, but tomorrow is *always* a new day and for someone like Brady, that could mean a whole new outlook on life. The damage has already been done, whether that be physical or emotional, and the way we manage it is to move forward, work on the idea that it will hopefully not be repeated, and by teaching him that dwelling on something bad is only going to cause destruction in the end. My fear will always be there, the worry that one day he will go to the river and never return home, and as his mum that's something I live with every day. I work through the issues we tackle as a family on a daily basis, sometimes on my own in my summer house or shut away in the studio, and sometimes with Mark or a friend or family member. No matter how old my boys are, they will always need me for something, however trivial, and I will always be there for them through thick and thin.

Brady wanted to come to terms with what happened that night on his own. But even he knows that he was treated unfairly, though I have vowed not to lay blame with either Zoe or him. They were two young people, enjoying spending time together, not really understanding the dangers of the world around them and how parents have a responsibility for their welfare. I do, however, find it difficult to sympathise with either of them in some ways, as they put us under a lot of strain that resulted in police being called, but I stand by my mantra and only want the best for Brady, just like Zoe's dad does for her. We haven't talked about it together since it happened. Brady knows I am always there for him should he ever want to discuss it. He loves unconditionally; he doesn't turn away from someone because they might be flawed. He gives everything of himself, for better or worse, and perhaps that does make him vulnerable, but it also makes him deserving of someone special to share his life with, someone who will understand him and know that the feelings he harbours are simply his way of caring and loving someone the way he thinks they deserve to be treated. I know that one day he will meet someone and protect them fiercely, he will treat his future partner like a queen, looking after her every whim. And this makes me even more concerned for him in some ways, because if that love isn't reciprocated or if the acceptance of "who" Brady is, isn't understood, it will hurt him deeply, and, of course, I don't want that for him. No parent would want that for their child.

I do actually believe that he was aware of the worry he was causing Mark and I, but he had little control over the way he behaved. Many people still don't understand the complexities of ADHD, or indeed any condition on the autism spectrum. Each person diagnosed with these hidden disabilities—because that's what they are, hidden—finds it difficult to control their emotions, to live and work on the same level as a neuro-typical person might behave. They take things very literally, for example, a friend of mine whose child is autistic told me a long time ago that her daughter asked her taxi driver who drove her to and from school each day, along with a special needs escort, how much they got paid. The driver and escort responded by saying, 'We get paid peanuts.' When the child was dropped off at home that night, she told her mum that she couldn't believe they were given peanuts as pay, and asked if it would have been salted or dry roasted. That is simply one in an ocean's worth of examples of how literally an autistic child thinks.

During those very difficult months of him being with Zoe, Brady went from that state of fight to flight, whenever his anxiety rose, which was usually when he'd be sat waiting for hours on end for Zoe to message him, or when he'd turn up at her house and she wouldn't be there. His compulsive nature caused him to just do something, whether it was right or wrong, and the consequences would be dealt with later, only Brady didn't think about the consequences, assuming there wouldn't be any. Near to the end of their relationship, we realised that telling him off and even trying to restrain him on one occasion simply wasn't working, and so we made the difficult choice to just talk to him as though he was an adult, making sure he knew for definite that he could contact us any time he wanted or needed to, and reiterating the need to stay safe. I found myself in his room on a daily basis removing blades and knives, and though I knew they'd find their way back to his room again, I wanted him to know that I was never going to give up on him. Ever.

He'd also lost a considerable amount of weight while it was all going on and had started to struggle physically. Walking miles every day, to and from Zoe's house and whenever they'd go on their treks through the woods and along the river was perhaps causing much of the weight loss, but his anxiety was also stopping him eating properly. I took him to the doctor at one point because I was so worried about how thin he was becoming, and with some advice and suggestions, we were able to overcome it. He eventually started to gain weight again, and once he'd managed to get Zoe out of his system, Mark and I noticed a big difference in his outlook; he was sleeping better and seemed to be focusing more on his school work, which was something of a great relief because within months, he would be sitting his GCSEs. I didn't know what the outcome would be, of course, and with everything he'd been through I honestly wasn't building my hopes up that his grades would get him into college. He didn't do an awful lot of studying, and hardly did any when he was seeing Zoe, but he did take those exams and just the fact he'd gone to school and sat in the hall in silence, concentrating for hours at a time, meant everything to me. I was so proud of him.

I remember the summer of 2022 when the results were in and I took him to the school to collect the envelope that would hopefully contain some good news. It felt like a very long drive at the time, and I'm not sure if I was more nervous than Brady. Students, parents and teachers were milling around the hall, opening big brown envelopes, some cheering, some looking on in bewilderment, others shaking their heads and perhaps wishing they'd studied harder. Brady was handed his envelope and held it for a moment, maybe scared to open it for fear of the truth inside.

I watched him slowly pull back the top flap and then gingerly pull out the two papers, looking at them with no expression that might tell me what the results could be. A couple of teachers came over to him and the headmaster asked Brady to hand over the papers to him, which he did. Then the next moment, everyone was smiling and congratulating him, saying things like,

'Well done,' and *'You've done great, Brady.'*

He looked up at me and the headmaster passed the papers to me. I scanned my eyes over them and simply couldn't help it; the tears came and I threw my arms around by very clever son, who'd gained the qualifications he needed to get him on the course he was determined to take. He wasn't too enamoured by the fact I'd hugged him in public, but right then I didn't care. His results were impressive, and I was utterly dumbfounded at how he'd managed it. He'd been through so many traumas in his short life, not least the last twelve months. He'd had a significant amount of time off for one thing or another, missed vital lessons, and let's not forget to mention the amount of time all kids had off school during the pandemic—going in for half a day then being sent home because a child in the school had reported a case of Covid in the family—it was all so surreal. But he'd done it. He was about to realise his dreams and start the next journey of his life with hope and determination as he studied his A-levels: Criminology, Ethics and Philosophy, and English. His intention being to get the grades needed to get him onto a course at Lincoln University where he will study for a degree in Criminology.

Once I'd calmed down and Brady had got over my outburst of enthusiasm in the way of embarrassing him with a hug, we made our way back to the car and got in. He connected his phone to the stereo and put his music on, and all the way home we sang at the tops of our voices to one of his favourite songs, *Wonderwall*. I was overwhelmed with pride for him. And he was overwhelmed with pride for himself, which is exactly what I had spent years helping him achieve.

Chapter Twenty

Hilda and Stan were familiar faces down at the allotments, a pair of Muscovy ducks destined to live their happy lives together free range along all their pals that consisted of hundreds of chickens and turkeys raised as produce rather than pets. It makes me laugh now knowing that as a little girl I would help my dad turn farm to fork, yet now I'm an avid vegetarian. So many hours were spent on the allotments, clearing up the bird coups, collecting (and dropping) eggs, digging and planting the veg then collecting in the crops when it was time to harvest...
"Cubbington Catch All"

You may remember, way back in Chapter Three, that I mentioned my obsession for watching early-morning sewing programmes on television before anyone else in the house was awake. I would sit by myself and absorb everything the presenters were saying on Craft TV, a regular live programme on the Sky channel Gemporia. In February 2021, a new live show was aired called *Sewing Street*, and that also captured my imagination. With a modern, appealing set and enthusiastic presenters whom engaged extremely well with their viewers, I got into the habit of taking the couple of hours a day that it was on air, to watch and listen, knowing this show was going to be huge; the next big thing to happen to anyone out there who

HUMMINGBIRDS AND KALEIDOSCOPES

was like me, a sewist with keen determination to grow. The first time I watched Stuart Hillard, I was hooked. When he made his appearances, the show had already increased its hours and popularity, and as a contestant on one of my favourite competitive creative shows, *The Great British Sewing Bee*, it was as though our paths had crossed somehow, albeit from a distance and only virtually.

He fascinated me from the outset, and became someone I could totally relate to. His expertise and professionalism in everything he did gave me great respect for him, and I totally wanted to learn from his instructions and demonstrations, and even bought his patterns. The following year, in the spring of 2022, I started to comment on his social media posts, striking up conversations with him and others posters, and that eventually led to private messages where we exchanged chit chat about my own personal designs. He was interested to hear about my creations and what I did, and when he asked me to send him photos of things I'd made, I was on cloud nine! I was probably a bit star struck if truth be told, and couldn't believe this television presenter who I watched regularly wanted to see what I'd made. I remember the first time I sent him some images of my designs and watched the little *send* icon zoom into the ether. I sat back and wondered if I'd get a reply, or even if he'd look. And when the three little dots started jumping about on the screen indicating that he was replying, I think I might have burst with excitement as well as nerves, all rolled into one.

Following our initial conversations, Stuart kindly agreed to look at some of the videos I'd previously uploaded to YouTube so he could see the way I presented myself, and I also told him of my idea to apply to Sewing Street as a demonstrator.

He was enthused by what I sent and as I read his message, I realised that I needn't have worried at all about his reaction. Instead of me wondering if I was kidding myself, his reply was telling me to write a letter of enquiry to Sewing Street and ask if they might be interested in working with me. I doubt I got much sleep that night, thinking about what I'd put in that letter and if they'd take me seriously. It was a big deal for me as it was paving out a new journey that I could maybe embark on and bring my business much more into the light. I'd had a shy personality and lack of confidence, not knowing what would happen one day to the next, wondering how, as a family, we'd get through the next ten, twenty, or even thirty years, and now I was being given a snippet of an opportunity to throw away all my doubts and fears and build myself up to someone I aspired to be.

I set about writing that letter and decided to make a short video of myself creating and talking to the camera whilst I did. I wanted whoever might be receiving my enquiry to be interested in what I could actually do creatively, not just read some words that might have made me look like another wannabe celebrity with dreams about being a TV personality one day. I wanted them to see how important sewing was, and still is, to me; I needed them to get to know me personally, albeit in a video that they'd only view on a screen. But I also knew that if I came across as confident, keen and well-spoken, not to mention knowledgeable, experienced and professional, that they'd see the person behind the pen, as well as the person behind the camera. That was who I needed to be; after all, if I was going to be successful, I would be putting myself forward to appear on live TV in front of a critical audience.

Suffice to say, when I received their reply, which I wasn't sure whether to expect or not, I could have danced on tables and sang from the rooftops, because they were inviting me for an interview on the 16th March—my birthday. *Was that specific date a sign?* I wondered. A new door was ajar, giving me a glimpse into a whole new world of creation, and if Stuart Hillard had been stood next to me when that email landed in my inbox, I probably would have flung my arms around him and kissed him! My husband got the brunt of my excitement instead, not that he complained, of course. Always supporting in whatever I choose to do, new ventures or existing ones, Mark was thrilled for me as were my parents, who insisted driving me to the studios in Redditch, where the interview would take place.

Choosing what to wear was probably just as exciting as the prospect of walking into the television studios. I went for one of my favourite designs by Tilly and the Buttons: a dress made in the most gorgeous soft pink fabric with random black polka dots all over, a round neck, sleeves that rested just above the elbow, and a garment that really flatters my figure. I accompanied it with one of my handmade necklaces in a silvery-grey and wore a black linen Ilford jacket over the top.

But the day before I was due to take the two-and-a-half-hour journey with Mum and Dad to hopefully secure the beginning of my new and exciting expedition into the world of television, my beloved rabbit, Lily, sadly died, leaving me utterly devastated. She was only two years old and had an awful accident that left her incapacitated. We kept her indoors for eight weeks to give her a chance to heal, but it was to no avail, and in the end she lost her battle and passed away. Knowing the interview—my big chance to shine—was the next day, was particularly difficult to comprehend after Lily's death, and I knew I'd need to be very brave if I was going to clinch this opportunity. I'd spent a few weeks going over my notes and rehearsing what I wanted to say, meticulously choosing a couple of items to take with me, praying the interviewers would be impressed. But that night before, I was truly heartbroken. I'd had the stuffing knocked out of me and I honestly didn't know if I would have the energy to travel down and sit in front of people without bursting into tears.

The morning of the interview dawned. I'd had a very restless night for many reasons, not least because I missed my beautiful and very mischievous furry friend, but because nerves were starting to take over, the thought of messing up and throwing away my one chance to show how much I wanted this. My eyes were bloodshot from lack of sleep and crying, and my skin looked like it needed an overhaul, so I got in the shower then laid out on the dressing table an array of face creams, smothering myself in anything and everything, desperate to look professional and completely determined.

Mum and Dad picked me up a little later and drove me to the studios, both of them chatting all the way down the motorway as I sat in the back going over what I'd rehearsed, trying not to imagine poor Lily bouncing around the garden, tormenting Bryn, the guinea pig. When we arrived, I got out of the car and walked confidently towards the main entrance, smoothing down my dress and readjusting my hair. I'd have to do, there was no going back now, and I went through the front doors, hoping the creams had worked their magic on my complexion. I introduced myself to the receptionist and was told to wait in the Green Room, a large open space with white walls and several windows overlooking the car park. A sofa and armchairs and a round, glass table occupied one side whilst other tables and chairs were dotted around, used by presenters to work at before they went on air. Soon after I sat down on the sofa, I was joined by Hayley and Ian, the key managers for the show and my interviewers. I remember feeling completely at ease as soon as I saw them both, smiling and welcoming, all thoughts of sadness now put to the back of my mind as they sat down in the two chairs opposite me and invited me to tell them about who I was.

It felt like I was chatting to two old friends, as they nodded their heads and changed their facial expressions to fit in with my self-explanation. I touched on my personal experiences as a mum to two boys and briefly serenaded them with how difficult it had been over the years, albeit rewarding to watch my sons grow, and I told them a little about Mark and how in sync we are, the way he continues to stand by me and encourage me to venture further out of my comfort zone, giving myself that much-needed confidence to progress. I mentioned my work at the university and the tutorials in my studio, meeting and working with incredibly talented people who taught me so much about their own lives. And all the time I was telling them my story, I felt their eagerness to know more, listening and engaging with me and making me realise these two highly-professional people were interested in me—Lucy Picksley, wife, mum, sewist, and a woman with ambition who wanted to go places. I'd taken with me two handmade bags and felt so proud to show them, explaining the stitching and what I'd done with each one, how I'd put an individual spin on each. One bag was the *Elizabeth*, which made me feel like my gran was with me, supporting me and egging me on like she always did, and the other was the *Warwick*, though at the time of the interview, I hadn't actually named it then. The bags weren't taken from my own patterns back then as I hadn't created any at that time, but they were my own bespoke creations that were eventually turned into my own patterns, with the Tale to Tell.

I was thrilled as I watched Hayley and Ian examine each bag, looking inside and tracing their hands around the fabric. They asked questions about them, wanting to know the names of the fabric and where I'd sourced it from, and when they suddenly announced they might like to create a new project on the show that would entice viewers to perhaps buy these fabrics that they hadn't come across before and make the bags for themselves, my pride just escalated ten-fold. Hayley explained how they could offer me one or two options if I was interested in working on the show, the first one being as a demonstrator where I would work with a pattern already produced and on the market, and I would make the item live on air. It was a fantastic opportunity and one I was more than keen to accept. But when she told me of another option, where they would use my designs on the show and develop them into patterns they could sell to their audience on TV, I nearly fell over with excitement! They were interested in pursuing my patterns—MY PATTERNS! It was a phenomenal offer and an opportunity I absolutely was not going to turn down.

It was a productive interview, I was sure of that, and I left after an hour of chatting, mostly informally, and shaking hands with each of them, feeling on a high. I'd surpassed cloud nine at this point, and even though I had no idea whether I would be invited back, and if my dreams would come true to one day be a part of Sewing Street, I got back to the car with a spring in my step, dying to relay every single minute of our meeting to Mum and Dad as we drove home. I rang Mark, of course, on that journey, telling him everything as well, and I imagine he detected the excitement in my voice, probably feeling relieved that it had gone so well after the difficult day I'd had previous to that one. The chance to be a demonstrator on live TV was perhaps something I'd only really thought of as a pipedream, but to have my own designs and patterns being on sale to a huge audience of passionate sewists and creators was something else entirely.

I knew the sadness would return when I walked back inside the house, as we needed to make a decision about what to do with Lily. And putting my fabulous experience at the studios to one side, Mark and I got to work digging a hole in the side border of our back garden, which would become her final resting place.

She had been much loved and as I'd done with all the animals we'd lost over the years, I chose a colourful plant to place over her grave: a beautiful pink camellia.

I went back to work and life carried on as normal, and then two weeks later I received an email from Hayley inviting me to the studios again, asking if I'd had a think about the options she'd offered. Without hesitation I wrote back to her to confirm I was definitely interested in demonstrating my own patterns on the show with a view to selling them. After a few more emails to discuss how we would move all this forward, Hayley gave me a date for my first appearance as a "Guest Designer" — 13th May 2022.

I thought about those two words, "Guest Designer", as they swam around my head, trying hard to let it all sink in. In a nutshell, they were keen for me to talk about my own patterns on air and give their viewers the opportunity to buy them. And I had to promote them in my own words, with the intention of making the people sat at home wanting new ideas of what to make, as intrigued, keen, and excited about creating from these patterns as I was. When I put the phone down, I sat down for a moment to recollect all the hours I'd spent sat on the sofa early in the morning before Mark, Brady and Haydn were up, making notes and listening intently to the presenters and their own guest designers as they talked their viewers through pattern instructions. I was one of those people who wanted to learn, who was determined to make something new from someone else's ideas and suggestions, and now I'd be on the other side of the camera helping the wannabe creators like me. It was initially only an hour's slot on a TV show, but it was a whole new opportunity that was opening up for me to be a part of a major craft programme, and this time, after feeling upset and missing my darling Lily, the tears pricking the back of my eyes were happy ones.

Chapter Twenty-One

Summer memories of Kinross Road are strong in my mind, despite us not living there that long. My best friend, Kathy, and I always favoured playing indoors and frequently had sleepovers, settling down in her sister's bedroom with a non-alcoholic snowball drink whilst Sarah from across the road was always guaranteed to have outdoor fun with water games in her back garden. It was the 1980s and I desperately wanted my hair perming, just like the pretty girls in Seventeen magazine. Unfortunately, my illusions were shattered when my mum applied a home perming kit and it left my hair in a tangle of tight curls, taking years to grow out ...
"Kinross"

I'd been given around eight weeks to create my own patterns, ones that would be displayed on the screen to all the viewers of Sewing Street. I'd never written a pattern before then as my designs had all been forged from my imagination; taking fabrics and materials and putting everything together to make something bespoke. The pressure was on now for me to come up with instructions and images, have them formatted into an attractive set of instructions that keen sewists would want to buy and create from. It wasn't just the wording I needed to get right, but the images, pictures and good quality photographs that would show the process of the make leading up to the end result. It was a huge undertaking and probably one I hadn't thought of so much before now, but it was also one I was one hundred per cent committed to achieving. I wanted to feel confident while standing in front of the camera live on air, talking about my designs as I demonstrated how to make them; it was important to me to make a success out of this opportunity I'd been given and my determination was very clear for all those around me to see. Mark and my parents were a massive help, as always, making me feel even more encouraged by the patterns as they began to come to life. I had to outsource areas of the work for the graphics in particular, as this was out of my expertise, but my family's support was second to none.

When I asked on my social media page for any volunteers to test my newly created patterns, I received five responses almost immediately from keen sewists eager to help. These people, also known as "testers", would work from a draft version of my pattern, using their own materials and fabrics, and spending their own time creating my design. It was a volunteer role, and their job was to flag up any errors in the pattern and anything that needed changing, adjusting, or even scrapping altogether. That process was quite challenging for me to endure as they sent masses of messages to me with their findings, and in some cases things that I'd missed out, which I have to admit, caused me to panic!

I took several deep breaths and a few steps back, realising that my excitement of this whole project had probably taken over the intricacies of getting the patterns just right, and turned to a designer I have a lot of respect for and whose patterns I've tested previously: Sewillow.

She gave me some very valuable advice that has stayed with me always:

> *'This is, in fact, the hardest part of the entire process, but it's better to get the glitches out of the way now knowing that at some point in the future you might well be lying on a beach and your phone will be pinging with sales for your greatly valued and admired pattern.'*

It was a challenge to get through the pattern-designing process, but with Sewillow's wise words of encouragement and my five testers, we eventually managed it in the end. They'd done me proud; I was immensely grateful to them all. I sent the final patterns to Hayley, who fortunately approved them both saying they were good to go. What a relief that was to hear! I didn't have to wait long before a large amount of fabric arrived on my doorstep, some that would be used to make up samples of the patterns, and some that would be saved for me to demonstrate with on the programme during my first guest appearance that was very fast approaching.

Because I was expected at the studio quite early in the morning, I made a reservation for my mum and me at a very nice hotel called Southcrest Manor, where I lay on the sumptuous king-sized bed, thoughts racing through my mind of what the following day would entail. I'd already received the packages of fabrics and had checked through all the deliveries, hoping there would be nothing missing, which there wasn't—much to my relief. A couple of days before I was due to travel down, I made up three Kinross cases and even though that made me feel positive about what was about to happen, it was scuppered somewhat the following day, when I received a text message telling me that Brady's ex-girlfriend was in town and had slept rough that previous night. Not being able to ignore it, I put my last-minute jobs to one side and helped Brady with this difficult situation, making phone calls and offering hugs, and all the time thinking, at the back of my mind, that I still hadn't finished making the bag I was supposed to be giving a live demonstration on in front of the viewers. I cried a little and wondered how I should time-manage this, and in the end I made the decision to plough my energy into myself for a change. This opportunity was something I'd strived for, and I needed to remind my tired mind that it was one massive point in my career that could really take off and benefit not just me, but the rest of the family, too.

That afternoon, Mum and I got in the car and began the drive to the hotel. It felt quite important to me at the time to stop off at my childhood home in Kinross Road, and I sat in the car for a little while before plucking up the courage to knock on the front door. The owner answered and I introduced Mum and me, perhaps feeling a little nervous that she wouldn't be interested in the fact this house held so many memories for me, but when she invited us both inside, I couldn't have been happier. It had been thirty-three years since I'd been in that house and I stood in my old bedroom looking at the walls and imagining my old posters of Simon Le Bon and other 80's classics staring pensively back at me. The room was now a nursery for the owner's son, Sean. But the feeling I felt when I soaked in the atmosphere of that room gave me all the healing vibes I needed after what had been a difficult morning.

I drove myself to the studio at 6.30 the following morning, feeling slightly nervous as I got out of the car, my arms loaded with fabric and patterns and all sorts of paraphernalia. But when the lovely presenter, John Scott, welcomed me literally with open arms, wrapping me in a warm hug, those nerves quickly vanished and the excitement of what awaited me started to take over. This was it. My big moment to share my designs and patterns with a vast audience and talk about my passion for creating. I couldn't believe it had finally happened, and I have to say I felt incredibly proud of myself when John gave me a tour of the building, pointing out the rules and regulations, showing me where everything was and chatting to me like we'd known each other for years. Once my tour was out of the way and John had made me feel completely at ease, he disappeared to the Dressing Room to get prepared for his appearance on the show, and I settled myself in the Green Room where I waited until I was called through to the studio at 9am.

The feeling as I entered into that space filled with cameras and mics and people lingering about with clipboards and bits of paper could only be described as euphoric. I'd gone from being the girl-next-door, who'd turned to sewing as a form of therapy to get through some very dark days, to a confident and determined woman standing in a studio with the words *On Air* hovering above the entrance on a neon sign, presenting my own designs to people who might just want to buy some of my patterns and create those items for themselves. My smile was as big as the buzz I felt when John introduced me into this world that I had so greatly admired and aspired to every Sunday morning in my living room. The most bizarre thing about that first appearance was, in my opinion, what I chose to wear. It was a very pretty, pale blue and white cotton top with flounce sleeves, and came to just above my waistline. I'd found it in a charity shop, but it hadn't been a top then; it had been a table cloth, for sale at the bargain price of fifty pence! I knew I could do something with the fabric as soon as I saw it, and when I matched it with a pair of my homemade Persephone jeans, it felt like the perfect combination in which to make my debut appearance on live TV.

John asked me about the top whilst we were chatting during my first hour and I felt ever so proud to tell him where it had come from and the fact all my clothes are handmade. Messages came flooding in for me, complimentary ones that John was kind enough to read out on air, from people who had tuned in and met the real Lucy Picksley for the first time. Some viewers were able to relate to me and to some of the stories I told whilst John and I chatted and I sewed at the same time, and the whole experience was absolutely incredible. In just twenty minutes of my first hour, my designs were sold out! Viewers had gone mad for the Warwick bag and it seemed they couldn't get enough of it, orders coming in at a rate of knots. John was so enthusiastic about having me on the show, as he is with everyone he meets, and at one point his genuine empathy was so overwhelming that he suddenly came over to me and once again wrapped me in an enormous bear hug. That first hour came to an end much too quickly, and I retreated from the cameras and went back to the Green Room until I was called back to do my second hour.

I'd taken the Lillington bag for that session, which also sold extremely well and made me beam with pride that people out there, watching me present my patterns and demonstrate how to make these bags, maybe while sitting in their own living rooms with a coffee and a notepad, were ordering and buying designs that I'd created. I got the feeling this was the start of something big for me, and I remember mentioning once or twice whilst on air about being invited back, something I hoped with every fibre of my being would happen.

I needn't have worried because I *was* invited back, and have since become a regular guest on Sewing Street, something I'm very grateful for as it gives me the chance to show off my patterns and sell them along with fabrics in the package, to budding sewists who have been impressed enough with the items I demonstrate that they want to make them, too. I've attended several social events over the past two years and feel I have made a true friend in John Scott. He's such a busy person, but he always has time to chat and to ask how I am, and of course to offer one of his wonderfully welcome bear hugs.

That door that was once ajar, giving me a glimpse into a new world of being creative and honing my skills further, was now wide open with a whole array of opportunities at my fingertips, and when people started to recognise me out and about, it was like my dreams hadn't only come true but had given me another reason to keep going. I've attended and demonstrated at live sewing shows since my regular slots on the programme, and it always humbles me to see an audience so large that some are left standing at the back and the sides because the seats have all been taken. It's a community I will always support, no matter where life takes me, and I make it my ongoing mission to help and guide anyone who asks for advice. So many eager sewists need to learn, just like I did, and they have to start somewhere. I want to be on hand to help them work through the challenges that may lie ahead.

Sitting on my sofa early on Sunday mornings watching live sewing shows is always something I will do because I still love to learn myself. There will always be something new I can scribble down in my notepad, someone else's idea that triggers me into wanting to try their design for myself or incorporate and adapt it into one of my own. There are many great sewists out there, very talented and skilled people who inspire me, and for them, along with my guest appearances, banter and demonstrations on Sewing Street, the future for my career gets brighter by the day.

Chapter Twenty-Two

Dad was ready, all wrapped up in his coat, boots, and flat-cap. The dogs were ready, tails wagging furiously, knowing they would be getting a good run out with a few treats along the way for good behaviour. On went the wellies and my big warm coat; it was time. My bag carried all the bits we needed to keep us going on our outing, the dogs were harnessed up and we were off. Field after field stood in front of us with nothing stopping us from getting there other than a busy road to cross. Sit and stay. The dogs waited until their next command to cross the road was uttered, where they knew a titbit would be gifted as a well-done for behaving so nicely...
"Leicester Lane"

One person I couldn't wait to tell about my news concerning my guest appearances on Sewing Street was my good friend Kay, the lady who owns Fabric Corner. She was, I'm sure, as excited as me as we hugged and squealed together, both of us knowing that this could become something "big". I'd been frequenting Kay's shop for the past five years and bought an inordinate amount of material from her, so I wanted her to be one of the first people to share my excitement with. I was thrilled when she offered her support, asking me to consider the shop to be my first stockist. It went without much thought when I nodded my head and gave her another hug. I remember thinking at the time if people I knew, who were familiar with my sewing passion, would think this woman from Warwick, who now lived in a large town in Lincolnshire with her husband and two sons, might have taken on more than she could handle. But I knew there and then that Kay would never think that of me.

So much so that, after my second appearance on Sewing Street, Kay offered to host an evening event in my honour and call it "Meet the Designer". *Me!* People would meet me, Lucy Picksley, the person who once upon a time had little confidence in herself and struggled to cope with the challenges of everyday life. But this was a new me—not a different Lucy, but a new and revitalised version of the woman I'd once been. My television appearances had given me confidence and made me realise that I had no problem about standing in front of people and talking about sewing and creating, and when Kay told me her idea for the event would entail me chatting informally to keen sewists about my patterns, even though I only had four completed by then, I jumped at it. The meet and greet part of the evening would start in Craftea Café next door, then hopefully attendees would meander to Fabric Corner and look around Kay's shop.

When the date of the event finally arrived, I pulled up in a space at the bus station car park opposite the café and the shop, gathered everything I'd bundled together, such as samples of my designs and, of course, the patterns I'd made—Warwick, Lillington, Stratford, and Kinross—then walked across the road to the café and got myself a cup of tea. I was quite early, as I wanted to be organised and ready for people to arrive, and when I sat at the table with my creations on display and a mug of tea in front of me, I started to panic a little at the thought of no one turning up. I would have been quite happy if five people came, in all honesty, and was beside myself with surprise when, as 6pm came round, that café was full to bursting with bums on seats and quite a few others having to stand at the sides due to the fact there were no chairs left! To say I was stunned was an understatement. I was completely overwhelmed. I smiled and made my way to an area of the café that had been set up for me to talk and share my patterns. All eyes were on me now, as I stood upfront, introduced myself, and talked openly about who I was, why I was there, and my wonderful new opportunities with Sewing Street.

Audience members asked me questions about being on TV, where did I get my ideas from, how did I bring the patterns to life, and my confidence just built and built as I gave them my answers and mentally thanked whoever was looking down on me for this insurmountable burst of pride I was experiencing. I'm sure it would have been Betty, of course.

I handed the samples I'd brought along to everyone, giving them the chance to have a good look and examine the stitching, then ask more questions about how I did this and that. Their own enthusiasm shone through as many told me they were keen to make the bag for themselves, using their own sewing machine at home. That cup of tea I'd ordered when I first went into the café never did get drunk!

After some more chatter and answering questions, we then went into Kay's shop and I offered my personal advice and experience to anyone who wanted help in buying fabric, mainly to go with my patterns. It was like

I was their own personal assistant and I think they got as much out of that as I did in helping them.

It was gone 8pm when I got home that night, and I was on an absolute high. Mark poured me a glass of wine as I walked through the door, I kicked off my shoes, put all my samples on the table, then sunk into the sofa with him and told him about the fabulous couple of hours I'd spent with a bunch of lovely people. I have a lot to thank Kay for, but that event meant so much to me. To be able to share my television experience, show off four of my patterns and let lots of budding enthusiasts peruse those bags gave me a huge amount of pleasure. Fabric Corner will always be my go-to shop, that's a given.

Chapter Twenty-Three

I'm a Pisces, born 16th March, and I am true to its characteristics. I have big feelings and strong reactions that tend to silence the intelligent part of my brain and activate the emotional side of me. I thought it was a problem for a long time, but now I tend to think I just wear my heart on my sleeve. My brothers, the twins, were born nine weeks' prematurely, and as Libras, they should possess an apparent sense of justice, great dependability, and trustworthiness. They were transferred to the Intensive Care Unit where my parents spent hours, days, and weeks wishing and willing on their survival ...

"Gemini"

In September 2022, it was time for Brady to start college and begin studying for his A-levels. Even though he was excited about this new phase in his life, he was, of course, a little nervous about what to expect. He quickly found his morning routine, get up, wash, dress, then leave the house and walk to the bus stop, which was on the opposite side of the road to the one he used for secondary school, meaning the journey would be in the opposite direction. But every morning, he got himself ready and left the house, always early and giving himself plenty of time to catch the bus. Missing it would have completely destroyed his day.

Hummingbirds and Kaleidoscopes

It wasn't long after he'd started there that we started to recognise the looks of discontent when he came in and when the phone rang and emails were landing in my inbox saying there were some concerns surrounding him, I guess I could be forgiven for closing my eyes and thinking about "Groundhog Day". To me, the issues weren't particularly crucial and as Brady had already proved he was intelligent enough to do this course, it became somewhat irritating when I was being told he sometimes didn't appear to engage in class. He was wearing earphones at his desk and he refused to take his hat off in the classroom. The earphones weren't allowed, and this was obviously a violation of the rules, but we knew that these concerns were simply Brady's way of wanting to hide away and not draw attention to himself. It wasn't going to stop him passing his exams at the end of the course, and surely that was what was much more important than whether he was wearing a hat or wasn't engaging as well as he might. His special needs might be a "hidden disability", but they needed to be understood, too. We talked to him about it and he explained that the volume was low on the earphones and was helping him to keep his anxiety levels low. This was a new journey for a young man with autism. His day-time routine had changed and for any child, whether they have special needs or not, moving into a differently-structured environment would always cause some level of stress.

We kept our eye on him and hoped it would get better, but within weeks of him being there, he told me he thought he might have made a mistake and wanted to transfer back to the school, where he could attend the sixth form in familiar surroundings with faces he knew. I agreed and made arrangements for him to leave the college and enrol back at the school, which we hoped would lessen his anxiety and give him back the safety net of what he was used to.

Unfortunately, it was a matter of days after being back at the school, albeit in sixth form, that he came home, completely distressed and pointed out that he hadn't realised how different the structure would be—that he much preferred the freedom that college offered and the more adult routine of it being slightly less structured, than that of a Monday to Friday routine in the school system where he was perhaps treated as a "pupil", rather than the sixteen-year-old who'd left school to attend further education in a separate location. He was lucky; I was able to get his place back at the college for him and have him reinstated on the A-level course he'd chosen to do.

He made a point from then on to try and settle in more, make new friends and adapt to the college way of life. He did make friends and once again showed his loyal and caring nature towards them, always wanting to help them and fix whatever issue they had going on. The problem was that many of them did have issues, and we noticed soon after he was back at college, that they started to offload those issues on Brady. It seemed like we'd gone back to the days of when Zoe was in his life. A friend needed him, and he ran to them. It didn't matter what time of day or night, Brady was there to help them. Unfortunately, this started happening more and more often when he was in class, and one friend would constantly message him saying he was having a crisis and Brady would just up and leave, feeling compelled to offer support. Leaving in the middle of a class was one thing, but then it came to the point when he just wouldn't attend at all, wanting instead to be there for whoever said they needed him.

The phone calls and emails started again from the college, telling us about Brady's absences and how he often walked out of the class for no apparent reason, failing to return. And we could see the downward spiral happening all over again; Brady just wanting to help someone in need and having no regard for himself or the consequences. It came to a head one day when he'd broken the rules too often, his sudden departures and absences would no longer be tolerated, and after just six months of starting his course, he was dismissed.

We couldn't believe it. All our boy had done was care for his friends, try to help them because that was his way. He'd gone above and beyond so many times to fix one of their issues, but it just went too far. We knew he'd truanted from class and shouldn't have walked out as though the lessons weren't important, but that was him. And something I chose to do was never use the word "expelled", because that would have made it sound like he'd done something wrong. He'd done nothing wrong. In Brady's world, he'd done everything right by supporting one of his friends. We can't punish someone for caring, and that was something Mark and I had drilled into Brady over the years.

We have many local authorities in this country and ours was pretty shoddy as far as helping special needs kids was concerned. Brady hadn't been granted an EHCP for his education—Education, Health and Care Plan—and he was literally on his own, trying to fumble about in an educational setting without any means of extra support, counselling, or special needs co-ordinators intervening and ensuring his years at college would be as trouble-free as possible. After all he'd been through at school, to have been expected to adapt into a neuro-typical environment was simply ridiculous. Now with no course to attend, he decided to appeal the decision. He wanted to learn, he wanted to do well and get the results in needed to get into Lincoln University, and so a date came through where we attended a very formal meeting before a panel of three members of staff. Mark and I accompanied him. He'd chosen to dress up for the occasion in a suit. He polished his shoes, and made sure he looked like someone to be taken seriously. He was asked questions and we felt he articulated himself extremely well, focusing mainly on the event that had led to his dismissal. Having an EHCP could probably have helped him; it would have been the document to outline his disability and therefore give credence to why he had done what he had. But it wasn't meant to be. The college ruled against Brady's appeal.

It isn't unknown for parents with special needs children to feel abandoned by the system, and that is exactly how we felt. We had been turned away. Making noise and pushing for something that was beyond the norm wasn't what the college needed. We were annoyed about how he'd been treated, but we were also annoyed at how we, as his parents, had been treated, too. Our son had been discriminated against once again for having special needs. He had gone against rules occasionally but had, in that appeal, tried so hard to make the staff understand why. We had also tried hard, explaining the difficulties he fought throughout his life, but they weren't interested. Brady wasn't your typical student who could just get on with his studies without anyone batting an eyelid. That was why it had been so important for him to be granted the EHCP. That document gives a wealth of information on the child's condition, instigating necessary support, stating *why* that support is needed, and a mass of detail about how life for a SEN child really is. Without it, there is nothing you can do to access that vital help. It's obvious to so many educational staff when something is "different" about a child; their behaviour, their skillset, their mindset will be enough to tell anyone who works with children that. So we knew that Brady's condition was simply being ignored. He didn't fit in, and perhaps because of all the horrendous events we'd already encountered that made him unlike his peers, I decided I needed to step up and do something about it.

I'm not a shouty person or someone who enters into confrontation lightly, but I am a mum, and like most mums, I won't rest until my child is happy. Brady had spent so long being far from happy that I wasn't going to put up with it anymore. I consulted a solicitor who specialised in disability law and asked his advice on a way forward. I was told that I did indeed have a case for discrimination and so I sat down with Brady and discussed this with him. I wanted him to be fully involved, knowing what would happen and be able to feel confident about speaking to experts and putting our case forward. But after a few conversations with him, Brady told me his decision was to put it behind him and move on. He was keen to work out what came next, knowing that he was no longer able to study for his A-levels, and knowing, too, that he would have to start thinking seriously about his future at university. I understood exactly why he'd made that decision and told him I would back him up every step of the way.

Between February and September 2023, Brady was at a loss with himself. He could have perhaps started somewhere else on a new course, but he found it very hard to cope with what had happened. His routine had been taken away and as a child who would find it difficult to have a change in circumstances for just one week, we knew that something needed to happen otherwise he may never get back into a positive frame of mind. During these months, we received no communication from the local authority whatsoever, and I approached Brady one day asking if he might like to start looking at volunteering work. I was thrilled when he agreed and after some searching around, phone calls and emails, I found him a part-time job, albeit volunteering, at a social enterprise establishment called Café Indie. Based in Scunthorpe, a bus ride away, the place is a coffee shop by day and a youth club-cum-music venue in the evenings. Brady went to meet the owner and was offered a few hours a week to start off, working in the coffee shop where it was quiet. They told him about boundaries and rules, most of which were straightforward, and said that as long as he told them if he wasn't going to be in, if he needed to leave early or arrive late, he was free to do so because this was not like a regimented school environment. It wasn't the perfect job for him, but he liked the location because he was able to continue his friendship with some of the kids he'd met at college, and even though they could be a bit unpredictable, this suited him.

He would sometimes walk home, several miles, and often along the route that always filled me with dread: the river that he used to disappear to in the dead of night, leaving me wondering if I'd ever see him again. But when he got in, he'd look refreshed; tired, but with a spring in his step.

As time was progressing, he often talked to Mark and I about his future and where his education lay, about the disappointment he'd felt after being dismissed from college. He was quite obviously fearful and even though he wanted to get back to studying again, he was anxious about starting at a new college. I looked into it for him and discovered a college of further education that I wanted to show him, but he was reluctant, had perhaps got himself into a state about the fact of starting again and maybe going through the awful scenario of not being able to settle and once more being dismissed. It was with a lot of talking and much unwillingness that I finally got him to come with me to the open day event where we were able to look around the campus and he could make the decision for himself whether he might like to give it another try. I could see his expression changing as we walked around the light and airy buildings, its atmosphere seeming so much different to that at the previous college. The staff were welcoming, chatting to us and eager to tell us about different courses and the college ethos. When Brady began telling one staff member about his dismissal, voicing his fears that it would put being accepted by another college in jeopardy, the man told him not to worry about it. He had a knowledge of autism and ADHD and listened to us with interest, nodding in all the right places and making us feel encouraged and very hopeful that this would be the right place for our eldest son.

The man went on to tell Brady that as he had no criminal convictions, there was no need to include it in his application and that as far as he was concerned, he was happy that Brady had left the college simply because it hadn't been the right place for him. And so he filled out the forms and we went home smiling, once more feeling positive about his education and his ambition to study criminology at university.

Brady was determined to make a go of it and so when the new term started in September, we went shopping together and he bought himself a selection of new clothes, these being smart jeans and shirts. He wanted to give a good impression from the outset. This was going to be a new Brady, not the kid who kept getting into trouble or spoke out without thinking, who bashed his fists against walls when he wasn't coping well. I saw a difference in him and could see that he was eager to adapt to a system that was, and most likely always will be, not capable of adapting to his needs, but we had to encourage him. This could be the making of him and that was something we absolutely needed to embrace.

And so, he began his routine again, getting up at 6.45am, walking into town to get the bus at 7.25am, and then arriving in Lincoln to start his day. Even when his lessons start at 11am, he still gets that early bus, which perhaps is unusual, especially for a teenager who'd normally spend every spare minute lying in bed.

But he'd spent nearly six months living in chaos with no set timetable and now he was desperate to get back to that regimented way of life again.

We've only ever told him to do his best, as that is, after all, the only thing we can hope for. We don't attend parents' evenings at the college because these events are too stressful for him and in my opinion, there's no point putting unnecessary stress on a young adult when he's coping okay. We rarely ask him about his course either, and don't pester him about grades and tests and try to make out that he should be doing better. We know he's doing fine. We also know he's never going to be a perfect student. But the fact he turns up and is studying, and wants to make a good impression is all we can ask of him.

Brady knows what he needs to do to get the grades to be accepted into university. If it takes him a few extra years to realise that ambition then so be it. The only person that can help him move forward and achieve the results required is Brady himself. We can tell him till we're blue in the face to do better, do this, do that, do anything *we* want him to do, but we won't do that. Not anymore.

A couple of months into his course, in November 2023, Brady announced to me that he had a terrible secret and needed help to sort it out. He also told me he wanted me to share this secret because it might help other young people and their parents understand the dangers of what he was doing.

He told me that for the past nine months, he had been addicted to smoking weed. Neither Mark or I had known; Brady had done a very good job of keeping this from us, but he felt our relationship was strong enough that he could confide in me and somehow me and his dad could get him the help he needed to cure his addiction. As he's got older, he's realised that we are always here for him, no matter what he's done, and the fact he had now told me and understood the implications it could have, made me see my boy as someone who was able to take responsibility for his own actions. Something I'd talked to Brady about over the years was how important it was that whenever he needed to talk and reach out, he should, and that didn't have to mean reaching out to myself or Mark. He'd reached out to Mr Quince when he was school, something that I was immensely proud of. But my pride for him increased ten-fold the following day, after little sleep from dwelling on what he'd told me, when I learned he had gone into college and approached a member of staff, asking for help.

That person listened to Brady and gave him information on places he could visit to get on the road to kicking this addiction and making a full recovery. That lunchtime, Brady walked to the other side of Lincoln city and entered an addiction clinic, telling the receptionist that he needed their help and why. He didn't tell me he was doing it, he just went himself, showing me that my beautiful boy was now maturing and becoming independent. As this book is being written, Brady still attends weekly sessions at the clinic where he has received a wealth of support. It's affected him so much that he is now thinking about looking into opportunities for work experience or volunteering to help others in the future. He recently mentioned where he wanted to be in his future career, and went on to tell me this:

'I want to be able to see a kid sat on a corridor floor, walk up and sit next to them and talk. I don't know what that job is but that's what I want to do.'

Perhaps he feels this way because of the endless support he's had from Mark and I, all the times we've told him we'll always be there for him and that he will never be, and should never feel alone. It goes without saying that I couldn't be more proud of him if I tried.

Chapter Twenty-Four

The earliest holiday I recall was heading off to Stratford Racecourse with our new tent; an orange and brown canvas construction, big enough for the five of us. My little brother hadn't been born then, so it was just me, Mum and Dad, and the twins. Stratford was just down the road from where we lived in Warwick, but that didn't matter. Mum and Dad were always busy, both worked hard to give me and my brothers a comfortable life, but holidays were a time when we could be together; quality time, when the alarm clocks were turned off and there was no schedule to respond to, a time we could all unwind in the sunshine together...
"Stratford"

In late 2022, when I was forty-six, I started to notice the early signs of menopause setting in. It's known as "peri-menopause" these days. It wasn't a pleasant time for me but I knew it would arrive at some point, and so I accepted this new phase in my life and tried to deal with it as best as I could. Talking about menopause has always been somewhat of a taboo subject for many women and I was a little cautious about discussing it with people, but Mark took it all in his stride and as usual became my rock, supporting me and helping me to cope with the changes my body was starting to experience. One of the things he did to help me was a complete surprise, one which left me feeling quite nervous yet exhilarated at the same time.

Hummingbirds and Kaleidoscopes

He booked a boudoir photo shoot for me and enlisted my best friend Milly to accompany me, mainly to hold my hand and settle my nerves! Before the day arrived, I was contacted by the owners and they went through all my inhibitions and insecurities, asking about my concerns and if I felt uncomfortable about anything; a certain pose or an outfit, or having too many people staring at me in clothes that wouldn't leave a lot to the imagination. They totally engaged with me and made me feel excited about the experience, rather than dreading the fact I'd be lying or sitting in an alien position to what I was perhaps used to and showing too much flesh to a constantly clicking camera. I was told to take something with me that I would be comfortable wearing, something I'd maybe worn before and felt flattered by. As a boudoir setting, it was inevitable my attire would be of the more skimpy variety, and when they said to also take items I could connect with from me being a designer and creator point of view, I decided to take my handmade quilt.

I was given a very warm welcome by the receptionist when I arrived, as he swooned over my handknit sweater, and when the stylist also admired it, it was decided one of the shots would be taken with me wearing it. Makeup and hair was, if I may say so myself, absolutely beautiful and transformed me to a woman I barely recognised. The makeup was heavy, but it had also been professionally applied to really enhance my features. I wouldn't normally have worn so much, plastered on for a purpose, but here I was, Lucy Picksley, mum, wife, designer, and now a rather sexy-looking woman approaching mid-life. I felt great, truly great, and the photos taken of me depicted that.

There were several "sets" where photos would be taken and my co-ordinator talked me through each one, explaining different images that were possible, all the time making me feel completely at ease. Milly was beyond excited to see the whole studio set-up, and built up a rapport with the photographer—her new-found role as "Arts Director" giving her an air of importance as she looked on in awe. My nerves had by now completely vanished as I became a model, just for an hour and a half, but posing in front of that camera on various items of furniture, including in a roll-top bath, was so much fun. They'd had me in all sorts of positions—clean, I might add—and had me wearing those seductive items of finery that made me feel completely at one with myself. A black lacey one-piece and black wet look leggings made up one outfit, then the lacey one-piece covered up with a waist-length, black leather jacket another, my legs bare as the lacey number rose high and flattering above my thighs.

When I left with a portfolio of twenty-one images for me to keep, chosen from one hundred, I felt alive. I felt as though I'd discovered a new Lucy, someone who didn't need to worry about age-related conditions and seeing another wrinkle when I looked in the mirror. I'd spent several months worrying about what was happening to the outside, when all along, that photoshoot made me realise it's the inside that truly counts. So long as I am happy with who I am, beauty comes from within—the old adage, *Beauty is only skin-deep*, certainly resonates with me now, though I did feel beautiful during that shoot and whenever I look at those images, it makes me see that woman who is completely fulfilled in

Hummingbirds and Kaleidoscopes

everything I do, something we should all remember to feel on a daily basis.

It was early 2023 when I took the plunge after a lot of consideration, contemplation, and bending Mark's ear, that I decided to get my tattoo extended up the right-hand side of my body. It had started off as a small rose back in the summer of 2000 when I went on a girls' weekend break to Blackpool. But as the years went by, that rose faded and left just a forlorn-looking weed doing very little because I always made sure it was covered up. I've always admired Milly's body artwork; she's had some beautifully-crafted tattoos inked on her skin, and it was she who encouraged me to go ahead and speak to a tattooist to have my weed replaced by something more substantial. She told me that when I'd had that rose designed at the bottom of my torso, it was because I was happy—perhaps a little drunk also—but she was right, I *was* happy and having a great time with my friends. It was a memory, and so that weed that had once been attached to a rose, would always remind me of that fabulous time we all had.

Now I needed something to remind me of later times in my life, times significant to me that I could look back on and ponder. That's when I got in touch with a very experienced tattooist, recommended by Milly, called Amie, and booked myself in for some extensive artwork. I was encouraged during the eight-month waiting time to think very carefully about the design I wanted, the importance of it and the meaning that it would have for me. My ideas were flowing and I started to make notes of events from my life, areas that were poignant, times

I wanted to think back on as I told myself how much my inner strength had got me through. I even went online and downloaded images to show Amie. I was determined to get this right and cherish the end result for the rest of my life.

I sent the images to the tattooist, and the day finally arrived when Mark drove me to Hull where her studio is based. She'd already got to work on a stunning design and when she showed me her illustration, I honestly couldn't have loved it any more than I did at that moment. It was perfect. It contained everything I wanted in exquisite detail, and I just knew that Milly had done good in recommending this very experienced designer to me. The first thing she asked me to do was lie down on the bed, offering me a blanket if I got cold, and I made myself comfortable, feeling a little apprehensive at the thought of those little needles piercing my skin. But it's a similar process to how a sewing machine works, and that made me relax a bit as I thought about my beautiful studio and the fabrics and my passion for all things creative.

I think it took about an hour and a half to finish. Amie told me I could get up and take a look in the full-length mirror, and I won't deny I felt nervous at the prospect of seeing my tattoo for the first time. I edged towards the mirror, perhaps somewhat cautiously. All I can say was that I was completely blown away. For all the right reasons! As I'd asked for, the design was predominantly black.

The tattoo starts off just beneath my navel of a relatively large, detailed hummingbird holding a needle and thread in its beak, its wings meticulously feathered as in a 3-D image. From there, branches and cherry blossom extend upwards in a swirl and this is to represent all the houses I lived in as a child, because in the garden of each one was a cherry blossom tree. This part of the tattoo will always remind me of those happy childhood memories, running around the garden and sitting under the trees having picnics and chatting to my brothers. As mentioned in Chapter Nine, it was in 2018 when I found coping with my everyday life had become too much, and I subsequently had a breakdown. To mark that occasion, which wasn't a happy one, of course, the tattoo also features a bee, but that design also represents me as a sewist—a *sewing bee*—and I had that included specifically to remind me that I got through a massively difficult time.

When I look at that bee, I tell myself I am good enough; that my confidence has grown and that now I can look back on the darker times with pride in myself for learning how to cope again.

You may have heard about the wonderful opportunity for young people called The Duke of Edinburgh Award. I was approached by a lovely young lady, Samantha*, who wanted to sew something to go towards achieving her Duke of Edinburgh Bronze. At just fifteen years old, Samantha had already experienced family loss and had the ambition to make something of her life that would hopefully help her come to terms with some of that grief. Her sewing skills for one so young were exceptional and I offered to help her create from my pattern called *Cubbington Catch All*. It wasn't quite as straightforward as just sewing the bag, however, as her tasks to achieve the award involved having to design the pattern again from scratch and to photograph every step of her development. My job was to write each process into a clear instruction.

We sat down together and agreed a plan of action, discussing which tasks she felt more confident in carrying out and where she would need more help from me. It didn't take long for us to complete all the tasks we were expected to achieve and it was quite obvious we made a great team. She took lots of photographs and recorded her progress on social media. It was very beneficial to me also because she was on a deadline and as those who know me will be aware, me and deadlines don't mix too well. So, in order to reach her goals, I had to speed up my process and make sure I wasn't lagging behind!

Samantha, suffice to say, brought a huge amount of joy to my daily sewing and made me smile so much as her wonderful personality left a warm feeling in the studio. It became obvious that she felt comfortable there, amongst the fabrics and sewing machines and my endless memorabilia. She was hurting and she needed guidance, and I truly believe our time spent together helped her realise how much of life she had before her and how many dreams she could make come true. A very aspirational teenager whom I would be honoured to work with again someday.

Name changed to protect privacy

Chapter Twenty-Five

A holiday to Milatos in Crete was planned; seven days of love and adventures with my husband, our first holiday alone in seventeen years. Our journey began with a curveball, however, as illness forced me to bed. Thankfully, we'd paid for an upgrade, so despite my being ill, our beautiful room looked out onto a private lush garden with vibrant colours and a plunge pool. On our final day, after spending three days in bed on my own, Mark took me to Sisi, a picturesque bay filled with calm and serenity. He gave me a piece of pretty glass he had found in the sand when he'd visited the bay on his own a few days previously, and as he handed it to me, he told me how lonely he'd felt without me by his side. A feeling he never wanted to feel again...
"Sisi"

As I reflect back on the last decade of my life, it is mainly with fondness, love, and a massive helping of hope within my heart. The good times outweigh the bad, as the darker days will always fade into the distance to make way for the light that will infinitely shine on our family. We've watched Haydn blossom into a beautiful soul, albeit now with a slight teenage attitude, one we parents must always expect from our offspring as they grow and discover a little more of this ever-changing world day after day. Our youngest boy occasionally tests our boundaries, and my patience, but he knows when he's gone too far, always backing down before things escalate and it becomes a war or words where there's no going back. He always apologises for saying something he probably didn't mean, more out of frustration and hormonal angst than a need to compete for our attention. It has become clear to both Mark and I that Haydn's greatest attribute is his sensitivity and ability to love, and this hugely extends to his older brother, Brady. He has seen Brady's flaws and dealt with the blows—in more ways than one—and even though we know our sons will argue again throughout their lives, we also know that they have a very deep and genuine adoration for each other. There have been highs and lows and losses and gains, some of them big and some of them small, but we will always offer our words of wisdom to each of our sons in their hour of need:

Every day is a new day.

I have spent several years now helping others, not only to sew their favourite designs and learn how to turn their ambitions into a keepsake, but by talking and listening and engaging in the best way I can. People come to me to get their latest woes off their chest; they sometimes sew while doing it and sometimes just sit in silence with a mug of tea and a plate of biscuits, hoping their words will come. I've watched many wonderfully talented and budding sewists come through my studio door wanting to leave with something to show their family and friends, often also leaving with a smile and a new dawn rising within their hearts. It's the same with my boys. I teach them, listen to them, engage with them my way, in a way that works for all of us. It might not be a way that works for all parents, but we've got through the last decade and come out the other side with another tale to tell.

In 2023, Brady and I had a heart-to-heart where he told me of his regrets towards the way he'd treated Haydn over the years. He was upset about his behaviour and felt a need to right the wrongs he'd dished out to his younger brother, almost praying that Haydn would understand. It was time for my eldest son to accept the responsibility of how he'd often made Haydn feel, still a boy yet one with such a grown-up head upon his shoulders.

It wasn't long after that conversation that I heard Brady walk across the landing and go into Haydn's bedroom, gently closing the door behind him. I stood quietly for a few moments, curious as to what my boys were doing, and what I heard through that closed door brought immediate tears to my eyes, leaving me hastily retreating downstairs, knowing this was a discussion two brothers needed to have by themselves. 'Listen up, Haydn,' Brady began, 'I want to say that I've been an awful brother to you…' and that was all I wanted to hear. It wasn't my place to intrude on their privacy, and certainly not to listen through a closed door to what Brady had obviously been so desperately eager to say. It broke my heart to hear my beautiful boy confess, but it meant the world to me knowing that he had most likely spent many hours sitting on his bed, deep in thought about what he would eventually say to ask for his brother's forgiveness. As I sat downstairs in the lounge, tears streaming down my face, the next thing I heard was both their footsteps on the landing, doing what they had always done best, play-fighting with light sabres. They were having fun together. I realised then that it wouldn't be the last time Brady felt the need to say sorry, or that Haydn would forgive and forget, but for that moment they were happy; brothers enjoying each other's company in the comfort of our family home.

Despite all the problems we've had with Brady and his failure at returning home either on time or at all, we no longer demand a curfew, and instead have had a well-meaning and serious discussion about him contacting us when he's out should he ever feel unsafe or discontent. It doesn't matter what time of day or night it is. Mark gets in the car even if it's three in the morning, and brings him home to where he belongs and where he's loved unconditionally. Brady will one day find his way; he will discover where he needs to be, with whom and why. He's a tremendously caring young man, and at the time of writing this he's now at the adult age of eighteen. Getting help for his weed addiction showed great strength and has been something we have coped with as a family. We hugged him and listened to him, decided to do everything we could to help him when he bravely said, 'I just need you to support me right now.'

Brady's struggles with anxiety are ongoing, they are part of who he is. But the more I learn about his condition—the autism and ADHD—the more confident I feel that we, as a unit, will steer him towards the right path and ensure he is fulfilled. We will never judge him. That isn't always easy, of course, as human beings it is our natural instinct to judge others. But he is our son, and if we can't offer him the support he will always need, it would be wrong to call us his parents.

In 2024, Mark and I celebrate our twentieth wedding anniversary. How much we've been through these past two decades almost beggars belief, but we have. We've been there, for richer, for poorer, in sickness and in health, and however stretched to the limits our marriage has been, those vows were meant with every fibre of our being. When one of us felt it almost impossible to cope, the other was there. I've locked myself away a thousand times to allow my head some space and my heart to beat again, and Mark's brought me endless cups of tea when he could see how a simple gesture would mean so much. He's driven me to hundreds of sewing shows and stood patiently in fabric stores, waiting in queues with me and hanging around whilst I choose fabrics and meticulously consider patterns I want to work with. He's taken the boys out from under my feet, knowing they might be bored and in need of a kick around in the park or an ice cream with a giant chocolate flake. He's been frustrated with me and sometimes lost some of that patience he's so famous for, but he's never allowed his own zest for life overcome mine, knowing we are two separate people with our own ideas and ambitions.

In our relationship, Mark doesn't need to "allow" me to strive for more; he gets me, he understands that I am that woman in his life with a massive thirst that needs to be quenched and my goalposts will be forever moved when I get too close. I have so many dreams still to pursue, and at the time of writing this book, some of those dreams are starting to come true. I know I have achieved a huge amount and for every single day I am grateful to all those around me for helping me realise the things that make me tick.

For me, life will always be a rollercoaster. I want to continue learning and meeting interesting people, working with anyone who wants my help not just to fulfil their latest enterprise, but to listen to their own tales to tell about life and work and family. We all need someone to be there for us in whatever capacity, and I know I'm one of the lucky ones who has this in droves. Being rich doesn't need to mean you have money in the bank or expensive paintings on the walls; you don't need to drive around in luxurious cars or go on extortionately-priced holidays. Being rich can also mean having a heart filled with love and a wealth of family and friends by your side. And as far as I'm concerned, that makes me one of the richest people in the world.

Twenty years: where have they gone? What do we have to show for them? I can answer that in just a few words by telling you we have everything to show for them, and I know we will have many more memories to make throughout our lifetime, not least with our two beautiful boys.

> *If I had a wish, one last wish, I'd spend it on you...*
> *Brady Picksley*
> *Aged 11½*

Acknowledgements

Collating my thoughts to prepare my Acknowledgements has been one of the toughest tasks in the process of developing this book, mostly because the thanks are so far-reaching it could be a book in itself. If you have not been detailed specifically then do not take offence, but know how grateful I am to you for whatever role you have played in my life so far.

If you have read my book you will probably have sensed my need for order and routine by now, so it won't come as a surprise that I split my thanks up into chunks.

Gran always told me that things happen for a reason, whilst my parents always told me that the sky was the limit. If I wanted something hard enough, then I would get it. With these positive mindsets and influences in my earlier years, it's no surprise really that I am a true believer of self-fulfilling prophecies and positive thinking. But I do want to thank my parents for always having my back, believing in me and supporting me with a listening ear and a box of tissues and a cuppa ready if I need them. They have seen the chaos of my family at its worst and have laughed with us and loved us all in easier times. For years my dad has been the one encouraging me to write a book and finally I felt I might just have something to share with the world. I hope you're right, Dad. I love you both so much.

I thank my gran, the person that's possibly had one of the biggest impacts on my life. Although not here, her presence is felt all around me, and during the writing process she surrounded me in my dreams, urging me on. I think she would be proud of me now.

In friendship I thank my ride or die girl Erica, for simply being just her. Such a wonderfully strong ambassador and role model for all the single parents out there looking after their kids, fighting fires and holding a job down. Erica, you are a truly amazing woman who has all the time in the world for me.

To Milly, my tough love, non-judgemental girlfriend, who reminds me to look after myself, stroke yarn and get away for girly spa days. Milly taught me that my role as a mum was to simply keep them alive and each day she would ask me, when things were really tough, if the boys were still alive and then she would congratulate me on this small but mighty win against the world.

There's Lou, of course. Kind hearted, sweet-natured Lou. The girl who works non-stop to support me to live my dreams, bringing my creative visions and ideas to life. You deserve only the best. Tom would have been so proud of you, my love x

It would be remiss of me not to mention the past 8 years working at the university in Health and Social Care and to all the people I have met along the way who have shared their personal stories with me. You have touched my heart in more ways than you might ever have imagined. You have trusted me with your deepest feelings and darkest truths and I have listened to you with nothing but admiration for the obstacles each of you has overcome. Every one of you has taught me a little more about who I want to be and for that I am eternally grateful.

The opportunities that I have had over the past few years have only been possible because I have learned to be self-confident and start to believe in myself. And this has come from every single person that I have taught to sew along the way. As I have taught you, you have shown me that I am worthy and good enough to be your teacher. Knowing that I have been a part of other people's success, no matter how big or small, has been rewarding for me and I just want you to know that I feel so proud.

Of course, I thank Sewing Street and the Gemporia Group for inviting me on to their TV screens and for the time they give me each and every month. Particular thanks go to Kerry, my scheduler; Hayley, Head of Sales & Programming; John Scott, Stuart Hillard, and Vicky Carroll for being fabulous to work with on screen. I have a ball every time I'm with you all.

A mention of gratitude also goes to the Craft Cotton Company for helping me realise my dream.

And so the time has come to thank my precious boys. Brady and Haydn, I love you boys so much. You two are all I ever wanted from life. To have you, and to give and receive your love. You have made me so proud in so many ways and I will never forget the random acts of kindness you show me when I least expect it. Haydn, don't ever stop being the creative fun-loving boy that talks far too much. That mouth might just get you somewhere in this world.

Brady, my special boy. With a heart so big it hurts you sometimes. Your feelings are big, and I know that you find life overwhelming and hard some days. But you're doing this, son. Small steps at a time. And I see them. Every single one of them, and I know that one day you will meet a girl who needs that big heart of yours to love her. I also know that your dream, to have a marriage like mine and your dad's, will be yours to have, too.

Mark. My Mark. You are my one. You always have been. Brady asked me to be nothing but honest in the writing of this book and so here it is. The last few lines. The past few months for the two of us have been hard. Harder than hard. In fact, we were both unsure we would make it. But when the decision came, to stay or go, I remembered our secret meet-up down the lane on the old wooden bench. Where we sat together and talked about how we wanted to grow old together. We thought life would be easy back then and that's not necessarily true. One thing is for sure, though, it's always easier when I have you by my side. Thank you for always holding the faith in me and not going too mad when I bring another cat home to the brood.

Finally, I give huge thanks to Kathryn Hall. The lady who has taken my deepest memories, read my deepest thoughts from journals and notes, and made sense of it all to become this book. If I was to start it all over again, I'd still choose you. And my appreciation to Lucy Sheffield for giving the book a final read through.

Printed in Great Britain
by Amazon